FREUD AND CULTURE

FREUD AND CULTURE

Eric Smadja

Psychoanalytic Ideas and Applications Series

Routledge
Taylor & Francis Group

LONDON AND NEW YORK

First published 2015 by Karnac Books Ltd.

Published 2018 by Routledge
2 Park Square, Milton Park, Abingdon, Oxon OX14 4RN
711 Third Avenue, New York, NY 10017, USA

Routledge is an imprint of the Taylor & Francis Group, an informa business

British Library Cataloguing in Publication Data

A C.I.P. for this book is available from the British Library

ISBN 9781782202080 (pbk)

Edited, designed and produced by The Studio Publishing Services Ltd
www.publishingservicesuk.co.uk
e-mail: studio@publishingservicesuk.co.uk

CONTENTS

ABOUT THE AUTHOR

Eric Smadja is a psychiatrist, a psychoanalyst, a member of the Société psychanalytique de Paris and of the International Psychoanalytical Association; a couples psychoanalyst and also an anthropologist, as well as associate member of the American Anthropological Association, and member of the Society for psychological anthropology.

He was awarded a prize by the International Psychoanalytical Association in 2007 for an "Exceptional Contribution made to psychoanalytical research".

He is the author of various books: *Laughter* (Presses Universitaires de France, 4th edition 2011); College Publications, 2013; *The Œdipus Complex, crystallizer of the debate between psychoanalysis and anthropology* (Presses Universitaires de France, 2009); *The Human Couple: A multidimensional history* (Presses Universitaires de France, 2011); and *Couples in Psychoanalysis* (Ed.) (Presses Universitaires de France, 2013).

The Publications Committee of the International Psychoanalytical Association continues, with this volume, the series "Psychoanalytic Ideas and Applications".

The aim of this series is to focus on the scientific production of significant authors whose works are outstanding contributions to the development of the psychoanalytic field and to set out relevant ideas and themes, generated during the history of psychoanalysis, that deserve to be known and discussed by present psychoanalysts.

The relationship between psychoanalytic ideas and their applications has to be put forward from the perspective of theory, clinical practice, technique, and research so as to maintain their validity for contemporary psychoanalysis.

The Publication Committee's objective is to share these ideas with the psychoanalytic community and with professionals in other related disciplines, in order to expand their knowledge and generate a productive interchange between the text and the reader.

Freud and Culture, authored by Eric Smadja (a well-known French psychoanalyst with strong and extensive interest in anthropology), is an original volume that deeply explores the path Freud went along while thinking—throughout his whole life—about culture and society according to his own and quite peculiar socio-anthropological point of view. Smadja examines Freud's opinions in the light of contemporary sociological and anthropological studies, trying to answer questions such as the nature and function of culture, its development, its importance in the human mental functioning, and the meaning of Freud's complex concept of *Kulturarbeit*. Eric Smadja's specific knowledge of the anthropological field, as well as his own psychoanalytic scholarship, make this volume unique and highly recommendable to psychoanalysts and to students of related disciplines.

Gennaro Saragnano
Series Editor
Chair, IPA Publications Committee

INTRODUCTION

Eric Smadja

Freud declared on several occasions in the course of his work that psychoanalysis was, or rather promised to be, a "bridge", a "link", and that in being so it acquires a mediating role between the medical sciences, psychopathology, and the mental sciences, the sciences of culture. Its very "essence" would consist of that bidirectional deployment. Indeed, from the time of *The Interpretation of Dreams* (Freud, 1900a), he maintained that the psychic processes at work in dream work were just as active in productions of symptoms as in cultural and social creations. As a consequence, psychoanalysis is not reducible to psychopathology, but also has things to say about normal psychic functioning and beyond that about socio-cultural productions.

In "Psycho-analysis", he wrote of not having had the

> space to allude to the applications of psycho-analysis, which originated ... in the sphere of medicine, to other departments of knowledge (such as Social Anthropology, the Study of Religion, Literary History and Education) where its influence is constantly increasing. It is enough to say that psycho-analysis, in its character of the psychology of the deepest, unconscious mental acts, promises to become the link between Psychiatry and all of these other branches of mental science. (Freud, 1926f, p. 269)

Hence the "twofold epistemological connection", pointed to by Paul-Laurent Assoun (Assoun, 1993), which would confer a certain *legitimacy* upon its practice in the socio-cultural field.

Of course, but what did Freud base his assertion on?

He considered that one may assume that the most general facts of unconscious psychic life discovered by psychoanalysis—such as infantile sexuality, drive conflicts, fantasies, the Oedipus complex, forms of repression and substitutive satisfactions, in particular—are present everywhere, may therefore also be found in the "most varied spheres of human mental activity", among which he pointed to the existence of "many surprising analogies" (Freud, 1924f, pp. 207, 205).

It is this very notion of "human mental activity", that of communities and peoples—whose unconscious processes and formations present analogies with individual psychic life—that authorises and legitimates Freud's move from individual psychology to mass psychology, within a perspective, however, common to that developed by Wilhelm Wundt in his Völkerpsychologie (Wundt, 1912). However, their treatment of the analogies would prove to be quite different from one another.

For example, the field of symbolism common to every individual—normal, dreaming, and neurotic—and to every culture, in fact, enabled Freud to grant psychoanalysis, its main concepts, and its techniques of investigation, a central position mid-way between psychopathology and the cultural sciences. Through the symbolic, connections are established between individual and collective human realities. It would be the same for religion, object of analogies with neurotic and psychotic individual formations.

In so doing, Freud would not recognise the distinctive, singular aspects of this socio-cultural reality either in its modes of functioning or in its productions, which differentiate it radically from individual psychic reality. He would create confusion between *the nature of the object* of his psychology of the masses or of peoples and that of the two disciplines contemporary with psychoanalysis, sociology and anthropology.

As a consequence, his methodology would principally consist of a *sudden, direct, massive transfer* of concepts deriving from individual psychology, that of dreams and neuroses, to the field of psychology of the masses, therefore, actually to the vast domain encompassing society, culture, civilisation, community, and the masses, something for which specialists in the social sciences as a whole would reproach him.

Nevertheless, Freud was conscious of the risks and difficulties of this methodology, something that he especially expressed in *Moses and Monotheism* (1939a), where he acknowledged that the "processes in the life of peoples which we are studying here are very similar to those familiar to us in psycho-pathology, but nevertheless not quite the same" (Freud, 1939a, p. 132).

He likewise considered it useless to conceive of the existence of a collective unconscious for these masses or peoples in view of the fact that he considered that "the content of the unconscious, indeed, is in any case a collective, universal property of mankind" (Freud, 1939a, p. 132).

It seems to me that associated with this is the statement that individual psychology is "also, right from the beginning, simultaneously" a form of social psychology owing to the significance accorded to the role played by the Other person all throughout the subject's life. Freud called these relations entertained with this Other person "social phenomena", the source of additional confusion in Freudian language with the terminology used by sociologists and anthropologists.

I would also like to bring up Freud's need to connect ontogenesis and phylogenesis—the childhood of the individual and the prehistory of peoples or the human race—on a fairly regular basis so as to explore both the individual psyche and the psyche of the masses and to make them intelligible.

Furthermore, it seems important to me to recall one of the reasons Freud was interested in this field of the sciences of culture, which was *that of helping it to eliminate the quality of "strangeness" of individual formations, those of neurotic symptoms or dreams, therefore of confirming the validity of the findings of psychoanalysis.* In contrast to Carl Gustav Jung, he could not, therefore, envision mutual input, either on the epistemological, methodological, or conceptual plane, something that must raise questions for us regarding his genuine interest for society and culture. And yet, he devoted numerous works to it. This means that he had, all the same, rather many other reasons for his interest, in particular, that concerning the major role played by society and culture—or formulated in other terms, in his meta-psychology, by "reality" and the "external world"—in the construction of each person's differentiated psychic apparatus determining his or her humanisation and conditioning his or her socialisation, something partially accounted for, according to my personal findings, by the notion of *Kulturarbeit* that he

introduced beginning with *The Interpretation of Dreams*. In fact, I think
that very early on he perceived and understood the relations of
interdependence and interpenetration between the two domains—
individual and collective, psychic and socio-cultural—without being
able *either to formulate them or conceptualise them in that way*, because he
was inspired by the individual–society antagonism prevailing in the
social and intellectual ideology of his time, something that can also
help us understand his *transition and his rough transfer of concepts of
individual psychology to mass psychology*.

I could, in addition, address my own reasons for interest in
Freudian socio-anthropological writings. They date back quite far and
are explained by my pluri-disciplinary training as a physician, psychiatrist, anthropologist, and psychoanalyst, to which I may add my
venturing into animal ethology during my studies of social anthropology–ethnology. I would readily add to that an old persistent, and
nonetheless stimulating series of questions about the so very complex
human reality encompassed by the term *culture*.

The interdisciplinary approach I have practised since the time of
my first book *Laughter* (Smadja, 1993) completely naturally led me to
inquire into the relations between psychoanalysis and anthropology
from a twofold perspective—historical and epistemological—via the
debate about the universality of the Oedipus complex that Freud initiated with *Totem and Taboo* (Freud, 1912–1913). This found expression
in my book *Le complexe d'Œdipe, cristallisateur du débat psychanalyse/
anthropologie* (Smadja, 2009), where I expressed a certain number of
reflections promoting understanding of the conflictual relations
between these two human sciences, as well as proposing some principles for interdisciplinary collaboration. But I had not yet explored the
Freudian conceptions of society and culture. In *Freud et la culture*
(Smadja, 2013), I finally realised this project and so it represents the
second part of a diptych, the first part of which is my work of 2009
mentioned above.

What society and what culture are we talking about?

Was it, in fact, *his* society, the Viennese society in which he grew
up, lived, and created psychoanalysis? As for *his* culture, we could distinguish, after the fashion of Didier Anzieu (cited by Jean Laplanche,

1989, p. 14), between the one he belonged to and the one that served as a reference for him. Thus, he belonged to Jewish culture, that of the liberal Viennese middle bourgeoisie, more specifically that of the scientific and medical milieu, and to the Germanic culture, while he readily made reference to Greco-Roman culture.

However, like every thinker of his time, he asked himself questions about western society and civilisation, experiencing critical periods generating "discontent" and change. Just as he was interested in historical and "primitive" societies from the evolutionist perspective of the British anthropologists of his time, which enabled him fabricate a myth telling of the conditions of the creation of human culture, of *culture in itself*, with its primordial institutions and social organisation, by establishing the Oedipus complex in its foundations.

So, when Freud dealt with society, culture, civilisation, the masses, or the community, I consider it necessary to take into consideration an inter-relationship between these different levels: contemporary Viennese and western, historical and primitive, finally the general categories of society, culture, and civilisation.

How did Freud depict culture and society in the course of his work, from his *Studies on Hysteria* (Freud, 1895d) up to *Moses and Monotheism* (Freud, 1939a), and *An Outline of Psycho-analysis* (Freud, 1940a)? How did he propose to define them? What vocabulary did he develop concerning culture and society? What terms did he particularly use to qualify them? What is its content? What constitutes a culture? What are its essential traits, its functions, its relationships with society and with nature, other aspects of "reality" or of the "external world". What account of it did he reconstruct (phylogenesis)? What would its essence be? What roles does it play in the development of each individual (ontogenesis), in the construction and functioning of his or her psyche? What about the notion of *Kulturarbeit*, which seems to me to play a particularly central role in his work, but which, rather curiously he never defined, and which I have *constructed* from a strictly Freudian perspective using his socio-anthropological writings and others outside that field?

To provide some answers to these questions, I invite readers to embark with me on a journey marked out by several dynamically interconnected stages.

So it is that Chapter One describes the Viennese society in which Freud lived and that produced some favourable political, economic,

and socio-cultural conditions making possible the birth of psycho-
analysis, his creation.

Chapter Two takes up and distinguishes between the often interchangeably used Freudian notions of community, society, and group
while first fitting them into the twofold category of "reality" and of
the "external world" within which "nature" figures. I shall particularly develop certain aspects: the "libidinal structure of organized
masses", social institutions, the notion of "social instinct", and of
"social feeling", but also that of social anxiety. Finally, I shall conclude
with relationships between psychoanalysis and society through the
themes of education, marriage, and the impact of psychoanalysis
upon society, its members, among them the patients, and the education of children in accordance with a psychoanalytical orientation as
proposed by Pfister.

Chapter Three is devoted to the Freudian conception of culture
and explores its different components from a twofold perspective,
synchronic and diachronic. In addition, I have deemed it interesting
and pertinent to my readers to provide an exhaustive presentation in
the Freudian spirit of the essential socio-cultural institutions constitutive of culture, and situated from the start within a functional relationship of interdependence: religion, morality, or ethics, law, and art.
However, I shall not expand upon other sectors of culture such as
myths, stories, and legends.

This is followed by a chapter devoted, on the one hand, to a
presentation of sociology and anthropology in Freud's time, therefore
of depictions of society and culture and their relationships as elaborated by the major specialists and founders of those disciplines, of
whom Freud unfortunately essentially knew nothing, with the exception of the British anthropologists, some of whose works he used,
mainly those of James Frazer and William Robertson Smith to confirm
his theses. On the other hand, it will be a matter of levelling both
direct and indirect criticisms aimed at certain Freudian themes, problems, and methodological aspects by sociologists and anthropologists
who were for the most part Freud's contemporaries. Apart from his
discourse on society, culture, his depiction of the relationships
between individual and society, or culture, they will especially deal
with his evolutionist thought, the symbolic, the notion of mass psyche,
but also the absence of linguistic considerations in his description of
culture and its institutions.

Finally, Chapter Five presents the construction of the notion of *Kulturarbeit*, an initial version of which I already elaborated in 2005–2006 and for which, moreover, I received the Psychoanalytic Research Exceptional Contribution Award from the International Psychoanalytical Association in 2007. This notion attests to the Freudian concern to understand, in particular, the impact of social phenomena and culture on the construction of the human psyche, of the humanisation of each individual, conditioning his or her socialisation through the intervention of psychic processes favoured, even required, by society, such as repression, sublimation of instincts, inhibition, symbolisation, the reversal of narcissistic impulses into impulses said to be "altruistic" or "social feelings", in particular. In addition, I initiate a critical discussion of this notion through recourse to the work of anthropologists and sociologists. It will be important to assess its heuristic value, for both the psychoanalytical and the socio-anthropological corpus.

Allow me to make one last remark concerning the translation of *Kultur*.

While Strachey translated it as "civilization"—something that readers will notice in the quotations from Freud's writings—for my part, I decided to translate it systematically by *culture*, because *culture* and *civilisation* correspond to different socio-cultural realities, and in that respect, the works of Emile Durkheim, Marcel Mauss, and Norbert Elias, in particular, support my decision.

The time has now come to set out to discover this Freudian territory . . .

CHAPTER ONE

Freud's society

In what society did Freud live and create psychoanalysis?

To answer this question, I take my inspiration from the Carl E. Schorske's remarkable book *Fin-De-Siecle Vienna. Politics and Culture* (Schorske, 1980).

Political aspects

In February–March of the year 1848, some years before Freud's birth, a first insurrectional, revolutionary wave was unleashed upon Europe, successively reaching France, Austria—with its neo-absolutist regime, essentially governed by Prince Metternich, Emperor Ferdinand I having been on the throne since 1835—Prussia, and, consequently, Vienna's satellite absolutist regimes in Italy and in Germany.

The Austrian Revolution was above all urban and grassroots, with liberal bourgeois and academic leadership. Czech and Hungarian "nations" rebelled as well. In an initial phase, the principal calls for reform came down to granting a constitution based on tax qualification and the recognition of fundamental freedoms. These liberal demands were coupled with national demands and demands for unity. Metternich's flight sanctioned the collapse of the absolutist and reactionary principles of the European States System of 1815. Emperor Ferdinand I was obliged to initiate work on a constitution. Then, after some months (May–August), a second wave of much more radical demands tried to impose the adoption of democratic and social reforms upon weak liberal regimes, and the national movements fell apart. Later, upon the announcement of measures taken against the young Magyar State, a fresh rebellion broke out in Vienna on 23 October, with the Viennese liberal democrats in solidarity with Hungarian revolutionaries. Incapable of ruling and discredited, Ferdinand I was obliged to abdicate on 2 December in favour of his nephew Francis Joseph, who initially re-established order in Austria by reinstating a repressive conservative regime.

Having finally come to power during the 1860s, the liberals of the bourgeois middle classes established a constitutional regime that lasted approximately forty years (1860–1900), but they only actually exercised this power for twenty years and initially had to share it with the aristocracy and the imperial bureaucracy. However, the retreat, actually the defeat, of this liberal regime came about with a rapidity unknown elsewhere in Europe, plunging Austrian society into a profound crisis. Its social base had actually always remained weak, confined to the German middle classes and German-speaking Jews living in the cities.

The liberals left their mark on State institutions through modifications made in keeping with their constitutional principles and the values of the middle classes. During the same period, they presided over the destinies of the city of Vienna, which became their political bastion, their economic capital, and the centre of influence of their intellectual life.

The principles and programmes of their liberal ideology systematically supplanted those of the aristocrats, whom they called "feudals". Thus the constitutional monarchy was to succeed the absolutism of the nobility and parliamentary centralism replace aristocratic federalism, just as science would be substituted for religion. The citizens of the empire of German nationality would be the mentors and tutors of the subject nationalities, which they would enlighten, rather than allowing them to stagnate in the state of uneducated serfs to which the "feudals" had reduced them. So nationality would ultimately become a principle of the cohesiveness of the people in a multinational state.

But Austrian society did not succeed in respecting those liberal "prescriptions" of order and progress. Over the course of the last quarter of the nineteenth century, this programme drawn up against the upper classes and the occurrence of the economic crash, brought about an explosion of the lower classes or "masses" made up of peasants, workers, craftspeople, the petty bourgeoisie, and Slavs. Indeed, far from rallying them to their cause, it instead succeeded in liberating those out of control social forces directed against itself, which then became the agents of widespread socio-political breakdown. Revolt also spread to the ranks of the middle classes.

Not all these new mass anti-liberal, national, ideological movements represented a radical break with the liberal's political culture. The non-German nationalist parties and the Social Democrats were certainly the closest to it, while the others—Pan-Germanism, the Christian Social Movement, and, in response to those two movements, Zionism—represented a much more clear-cut break. Georg von Schoenerer, leader of the Pan-Germanists, and Karl Lueger, leader of the Christian Social Party, were to become the inspirers and political models of Adolf Hitler. A third individual, Theodor Herzl, broke new ground by offering Jews the most efficacious and the most enticing political answer ever provided to the reign of anti-Semite terror.

Schoenerer, Lueger, and Herzl all began their political careers in the liberal fold. Then they broke with it to organise the masses neglected or rejected by mainstream liberalism. They also had a particular gift for responding to the social and spiritual aspirations of their followers.

Schoenerer organised the extremist German nationalists in 1882 and had them adopt a virulent brand of anti-Semitism that became one of the principal forces dissolving political life in Austria. His great success was to have transformed the tradition of the Old Left into an ideology of the New Right. He metamorphosed democratic, *grossdeutsch* nationalism into racist Pan-Germanism.

Meanwhile, Lueger did the opposite. He transformed an ideology of the old right-wing—political Austrian Catholicism—into an ideology of the New Left, Christian Socialism.

Herzl's plan was to make a liberal utopia, Zionism, into a concrete reality for his people, not based on rational arguments, but according to a creation of the imagination, while providing the response needed to the terrifying work of creative destruction undertaken by Schoenerer and Lueger.

In fact, towards the end of the century, the Jews themselves, whom Austro-liberalism had emancipated, had accorded opportunities for success and assimilation into the modern world, had begun to turn away from their benefactors. The collapse of liberalism made victims of the Jews, and the most attractive response to their oppression was the flight to a national homeland proposed by Zionism. Indeed, the fortunes of liberal ideas and the fate of the Jews became identified. Thus, to the extent that the nationalists sought to weaken the central power of the monarchy to their own advantage, the Jews were attacked by all the nationalities combined.

Urban middle-class Jews held erudite, refined bourgeois culture in high esteem, because the world of commerce had left an even deeper imprint there than upon any other. Years later, they would seek to escape the commercial activities with which they had always been identified. Assimilation through culture, forsaking economic professions for intellectual vocations, was then but a second stage in the upward social mobility of the bourgeois middle classes. This was precisely the case of Freud and his family.

During the 1890s, sometimes using the urns, sometimes parliamentary obstruction, sometimes mass demonstrations and rioting, the anti-liberal movements paralysed the State and relieved liberals of the responsibilities they had assumed only thirty years earlier. The position of the liberal upper bourgeoisie thus became most paradoxical. As its wealth grew, political power eluded it, while its professional and cultural pre-eminence in the Empire remained almost entirely unchallenged. It came to reign without being able to govern; felt a strange sense of its superiority mixed with impotence. According to Schorske, it was this ambiguity that would find expression in the products of the new aesthetic movement.

In 1895, Vienna, bastion of liberalism *par excellence*, was swept up in a Christian Social tidal wave. Backed by the Catholic hierarchy, Emperor Francis Joseph refused to ratify the election of the Catholic anti-Semite Karl Lueger to City Hall. But, two years later, the tide could no longer be stemmed. The Emperor bowed to the electorate and ratified Lueger's election as mayor. The Christian Social party would reign for ten years in Vienna. Its politics combined everything horrifying to liberals: anti-Semitism, clericalism, and municipal socialism. By around 1900, the liberals were defeated as a parliamentary force on the national level as well. They would never rise from the ashes. They had been crushed by the Christian, anti-Semitic, socialist, and nationalist modern mass movements.

This defeat had profound psychological repercussions. More than showing liberalism's decadence, it demonstrated its impotence. The ideology of progress seemed to have seen its day. "Anxiety, impotence, a heightened awareness of the brutality of social existence: these features assumed new centrality in a social climate where the creed of liberalism was being shattered by events," comments Schorske. (Schorske, 1980, p. 6)

The Viennese elite, the aristocracy, and liberal bourgeois culture

Schorske has us observe the "socially circumscribed character of the Viennese cultural elite, with its unusual combination of provincialism and cosmopolitanism, of traditionalism and modernism" (Schorske, 1980, p. xxvii). In comparison to London, Paris, or Berlin, where academics, art critics, journalists, writers, politicians, or intellectuals frequented relatively isolated professional circles and hardly knew one another, the cohesiveness of the elite was strong in Vienna up until 1900. Thus, the "salon and the café retained their vitality as institutions where intellectuals of different kinds shared ideas and values with each other and still mingled with a business and professional elite proud of its general education and artistic culture" (Schorske, 1980, p. xxvii). This "second Viennese society"—where lives and careers could intertwine, as Freud's life and his appointment as a professor did—was the product of a convergence of politics and culture. As a result, the alienation of the intellectuals in relation to other categories of the elite, and the development of an avant-garde "subculture" cut off from the political, ethical, and aesthetic values of the *haute bourgeoisie* occurred later in Vienna than in other capitals of European culture, even though they proved to be more irremediable and pronounced. It was only during the last ten years before the First World War that intellectuals appeared alien to society as a whole.

Profoundly Catholic, aristocratic culture was plastic and sensual. The representational arts, music, theatre, and architecture were central to its tradition. Nature was perceived as a scene of happiness and as a gift from God to be glorified by the arts, while for the bourgeoisie it was but a sphere of action to be mastered by imposing divine law.

This Austrian culture was, therefore, primarily aesthetic, unlike the moralising, philosophical, scientific German culture.

Moreover, unlike other European aristocracies, it was almost impossible for the Austrian bourgeoisie to gain entry into the hereditary aristocracy, also marked by a strong sense of caste.

Liberal bourgeois culture believed that humans were rational beings who would master nature through science and themselves through morality, two conditions necessary to the creation of a just society. Let us take a look at its two sets of values dominant during the second half of the nineteenth century: moral and scientific values, on the one hand; aesthetic values, on the other.

The ethico-scientific culture of the Viennese *haute bourgeoisie* scarcely differed from the diverse expressions of the "Victorianism" in vogue in other countries of Europe. When it came to morality, it was sure of its righteousness, virtuous and repressive. In politics, it was concerned about seeing the law prevail and about subjugating the social order and individual rights to it, just as intellectually it intended to make the body subject to the mind and to advocate a modern Voltairism: the path to social progress was to go by way of science, education of the masses or *Bildung* (in other words, the development of the life of the mind and personality of individuals, but would evolve towards a higher culture assuring a social position), and hard work. We find here certain ideas vigorously defended by Freud.

Sciences and history were prized for their social utility as keys to progress. But on the scale of bourgeois values, the arts enjoyed a position almost as important as rational knowledge. Why was this?

Art was, in fact, intimately tied to social status, especially in Austria. If it was almost impossible for anybody to gain entry into the hereditary aristocracy, the aristocracy of the spirit was open to anyone possessed of ambition, abilities, and will. Museums, theatres, and a university education could bring culture to everyone and lead to the forgetting of "lowly origins". The idea that art could play such a central role in society had a great impact on its own dynamism.

Beginning in about 1860, two generations of children of the *bonne bourgeoisie* were raised in the museums, theatres, and concert halls of the new *Ringstrasse*. Their culture was not, as it was for their parents, a source of pleasure or a symbol of social status, but the very essence of their lives. While the earlier generation's upbringing had oriented it towards professional, social vocations, the new generation immersed itself in culture out of love of art.

During the 1890s, and later on at the turn of the twentieth century, Viennese society was utterly disintegrating under the impact of the crisis liberalism was undergoing and the threats brought to bear by the mass political movements. They considerably undermined the confidence that liberals traditionally placed in their own legacy of rationality, moral law, and progress. A culture of feelings was coming into existence alongside the moralistic culture that had traditionally been that of the European bourgeoisie. But the former would subvert the latter through its amorality and shape the mentality of bourgeois intellectuals and artists, as well as sharpening their sensibilities. It was also the source of their problems. In this conjunction of socio-political circumstances in Vienna, *homo rationalis* had to step aside to make way for a richer, but more dangerous and mercurial individual, *homo psychologicus*, who mixed instinct and feeling with reason. It is this creature that people tended to make the measure of all things. The lot of individuals was the concern of its best writers, as well as its artists and psychologists. A new vision of human beings was drawn from that. And Freud's creation, psychoanalysis, came into existence in this turbulent socio-cultural and political matrix of *"fin-de-siècle"* Vienna.

In addition, having internalised a very individuated, distorted, secularised form of the aestheticism and sensuality of the aristocratic culture of grace, the cultivated bourgeoisie no longer saw art as an ornament, but as an essence and expression, even the very source, of values, then as a haven in the midst of this social and political disaster. That aesthetic heritage was thus transformed into a culture of hypersensitivity, a tortured hedonism. In Austria, the aestheticism that took the form of a revolt against bourgeois culture everywhere else in Europe became the means of expressing that very culture.

Adding to the complexity of the situation, the liberal intelligentsia never completely abandoned a traditional characteristic of its ideology, the primacy of ethico-scientific law. For this reason, in Austria's finest examples, the claims made for art and the life of the senses were always coupled with a paralysing feeling of guilt.

The city of Vienna, the Ringstrasse, and the birth of form of urban modernity

From the time they came to power, the liberals undertook to reshape Vienna in accordance with their conceptions, and by the time they were ousted at the end of the century, they had to a great extent transformed the face of the capital. At the heart of this urban reconstruction, the *Ringstrasse*, a vast complex of public buildings and private residences, occupied a wide belt of land that separated the old city from the suburbs. This architectural complex reflected more a concern for municipal development than a recording of liberal values in stone and space.

The liberal municipal government was able to provide Vienna with the means technically necessary for the absorption of a rapidly growing population in relatively good conditions of health and safety and without undue disruption. Rapid demographic growth took place during the 1850s, which saw an influx of population into a city of half-a-million inhabitants where the dearth of housing gave cause for concern. From 1840 to 1870, both Vienna's population and the number of its economic enterprises doubled.

The year 1873 saw the opening of the first city hospital, which symbolised the municipality's wish to discharge in the name of medicine the responsibilities that the Church had assumed up until then in the name of charity. Thanks to the public health system, the principal epidemics disappeared from the city. Only tuberculosis continued to strike the lower class neighbourhoods. Unlike Berlin and the industrial cities of the north, expanding Vienna maintained its attachment to green spaces, a legacy of the Baroque era, responsive then to physiological and organic ideas characteristic of the nineteenth century.

Built on former military terrain, this transformation took place in several stages, from 1861 to 1865, then from 1868 to 1873. However, the military left their mark on this *Ringstrasse*, for it was designed as a wide thoroughfare encircling the city centre intended to facilitate the rapid deployment of troops and equipment into dangerous areas. In this respect, military designs were compatible with those of civilians, who desired an imposing boulevard, so that the Ring was both circular in form and a monumental in scale.

The political changes inevitably sharpened the contrast between the old city and the Ring area, the former still dominated by symbols of first two "estates": the baroque Hofburg, the residence of the Emperor, the elegant palaces of the aristocracy, the Gothic cathedral of Saint Stephen, an abundance of smaller churches scattered throughout its narrow streets. In the new *Ringstrasse*, the third estate celebrated in architecture the victory of constitutional law over imperial force and that of secular culture over religious faith. The centres of constitutional government and higher culture dominated there, among them: the *Reichsrat* or parliament; the *Rathaus* or City Hall; the university; the *Burgtheater* or Court Theatre. Nevertheless, if in law and science the triumphant bourgeoisie passionately asserted its independence from the past, each time it engraved its values in stone, it borrowed the historical style most apt to express each building's function from the artistic language of earlier centuries.

Up until the fall of the monarchy, and despite the development of villa neighbourhoods in the city's suburbs, the Ring attracted all of Vienna's elite, without exception: the aristocracy, leaders in commerce, civil servants, and the liberal professions.

In 1893, the architect Otto Wagner won a competition for a new development plan for Vienna, the most substantial one envisaged since the creation of the *Ringstrasse*. He would develop a functional, rationalistic conception of architecture. This time, the city council emphasised the non-aesthetic aspects of urban expansion: communications, sanitary and social organisations, and plans for land use. The idea that transportation was the key to urban growth played a pre-eminent role in Wagner's plan. He envisaged four circumferential belts of roads and railways, the first of which would be the Ring, which would be intersected by radial thoroughfares. Business concerns and its needs for profitability, economy, and efficiency played a predominant role in modern life as compared to life in earlier times.

Wagner ultimately wanted to make Vienna into a "functional whole" in the service of a rationally organised urban civilisation and he demanded a new aesthetic expressing the reality of the hectic, functional capitalistic society that he willingly embraced. Thus, he seemed to be a modernist par excellence. In his search for an artistic language adapted to his times, he found allies in the young generation of Viennese artists and intellectuals who were then the pioneers of twentieth century culture, those of the *Secession*, which I am going to present.

The modernist movements

Beginning in 1890, the first modernist movements made their appearance in most fields within the very critical socio-political context I have already depicted. Austrians engaged in a process of critically reformulating and subversively transforming their traditions. The term *die Jungen* (the young), used to designate innovators revolting against classical liberalism and its value system, spread into all spheres of society, especially into literary circles, among artists and architects who seized upon art nouveau to leave a characteristically Austrian imprint upon it.

Thus *Jung-Wien* was the literary movement that, around 1890, combatted the moralising of nineteenth century literature, calling for more sociological and psychological truth, and sexual truth in particular. In quite different ways, Arthur Schnitzler (1862–1931) and Hugo von Hofmannsthal (1874–1929) had to deal with the dying aesthetic, political, and moral culture of *fin-de-siècle* Vienna and the dissolution of the classical liberal ideal of humankind. They bore witness to the advent of *homo psychologicus* amid the ruins of the old culture.

Meanwhile, within the *Künstlergenossenschaft*, the principal association of artists, *die Jungen* combined efforts to reject the classical realist tradition reigning at the time and to promote an experimental attitude in painting in search of the true essence of the modern person. To this end, these young Viennese found inspiration in the most artistically advanced countries. Though a young master of the old school, Gustav Klimt (1862–1918) quickly came to head the *Jungen* revolt in the plastic arts. In 1897, it was with him that they left the official association of artists to found the *Secession*. In the Viennese cultural situation, it was characteristic for the new association's ideology to owe as much to literary figures and left-wing liberals as to artists.

The *Secession* therefore proposed to tell the *truth* about modern people, in Otto Wagner's words, "to show modern man his true face". Vehemently anti-historical, the *Secession* consciously freed the imagination from any fetters to create a style liberated from the past. But more than anything the *Secession* was in search of a style. It maintained that, having become a surrogate religion, art had to provide people with a haven sheltering them from the tensions of modern life.

Its motto was "To the age its art, to art its freedom". *Ver Sacrum* (*Sacred Spring*), the movement's magazine, also expressed its profound determination to regenerate art in Austria, and Austria through art. Thus, cultural renewal and personal introspection, the identity of the modern person, and a refuge from modern life, truth, and pleasure, all these notions contained in the Secessionists' manifestos conjured up many contradictions compatible with a single aim: a common rejection of the nineteenth century's certainties.

Gustav Klimt was the president and uncontested leader of this movement. With Wagner, he was persuaded of the need to proclaim a new function for art even before the means of expressing it had been found. He was a perfect illustration of the socio-cultural context into which psychoanalysis was also born. He, too, found himself facing a period of historical transition, experiencing along with other artists and intellectuals a profound collective crisis. Like Gustav Malher, his ideas evolved in intellectual and artistic social circles that were open to one another and thoroughly permeated with Wagnerian and Nietzschean ideology.

For Klimt, modernity's quest was essentially the search for *homo psychologicus*, who appeared in literature at the beginning of the 1890s. Klimt used classical symbols, Greek myths, as a metaphorical medium for his exploration of instincts and in so doing depicted the psychic suffering of modern people helplessly caught up in the flow of destiny.

It fell to the new generation of expressionists to deepen their commitment to this approach, which Klimt had abandoned in about 1908 to return to the classical historical painting that had brought him fame in his early days among the bourgeoisie of the Ring.

It is to be noted that for four years, from 1900 to 1904, the government tried to save Austria by means of the economy and culture. It was within this context of politics transcending nationalities that the encouragement that the Secession received from the State is to be understood.

Expressionism: Oskar Kokoschka (1886–1980) and Arnold Schoenberg (1874–1951)

In the Austria of 1908, the neo-classical and art deco trends celebrated their triumph during the great public retrospective exhibition, *Kunstschau 1908*. These artists had wanted to unify the fine arts and the applied arts. This Kunstschau group associated the ideal of *homo aestheticus* with a special interest in the creative and artistic abilities of children, thanks to which the young Kokoschka had an opportunity to participate in it, something that, paradoxically, through him detonated the expressionist explosion.

Kokoschka's first revolution was to reintroduce a raw, unvarnished approach to instincts into painting, pursuing the exploration that Klimt and the *Secession* had so brazenly begun, while his second revolution, beginning in 1908, of which all his portraits are an example, involved connecting a revelation of inner life to a concrete personal experience.

In the same year of 1908, Arnold Schoenberg was, in Schorske's words, "laying the powder train for the explosion in music" (Schorske, 1980, p. 350).

Like Richard Strauss and many other composers of the time, Schoenberg found in Richard Wagner's music a major source of inspiration as well as very "fin-de-siècle" themes: erotic affirmation and the dissolution of boundaries between the ego and the world. Like Kokoschka, he accorded his feelings and instincts great value. Individualistic, resolutely bourgeois, he fought against society and its restrictive aesthetic forms for "the rights of the psyche". An expressionist interested in psychological life, he placed those listening to his music in the presence of an art whose ostensible structure was broken, an art fully expressing the feelings of human beings cast adrift, vulnerable in a universe that was eluding their grasp, but he was able to posit the subliminal, inaudible world of a rational order that would lend unity to chaos.

Among the artists of the new generation, Kokoschka's and Schoenberg's clean art directly exposed the instinctual and psychological truths that their precursors had drawn out of the shadows, but had only been able to render through indirect allegorising. And they grounded their innovative power in a clear, explicit affirmation of primacy of the ego.

As for Freud

So Freud came of age amid the new liberalism that triumphed in Austria during the 1860s. In that society, he also embraced the political values he retained throughout his life—admiration for Napoleon, who had conquered backward Central Europe, contempt for the monarchy and the aristocracy, unswerving admiration for England; and above all, hostility towards religion and especially towards Rome—but also the bourgeois values of commitment to law and the rights of individuals, the triumph of scientific rationality, of *Bildung* and the meaning of work, conditions of social and human progress. Like most cultivated Austrians of his generation, Freud was sustained by classical culture.

But, owing to his family background, his convictions, and his socio-cultural origins, Freud also belonged to the social group most threatened by the anti-liberal mass movements: liberal Viennese Jews. He anxiously watched the coming to power of the New Right, both in Austria and abroad, and Karl Lueger was his *bête noire*. The fresh outbreak of anti-Semitism badly affected his already hurting professional life. The academic promotion of Jews at the faculty of medicine grew all the more difficult during the years of crisis after 1897. The social discontent, the disillusionment with liberal values and major themes expressed by the writers and artists, such as *homo psychologicus*, his anxiety, suffering, and mourning of the loss of liberal ideals, but also his revolt against bourgeois sexual morality, with a need to express the eroticism as borne witness to by writers and artists, as well as the advent of modern human beings, surely figured among the factors conditioning the creation of psychoanalysis.

And then the First World War broke out in 1914, which was a period of serious, profound crisis for western science and rationality, and especially for Freud's profoundly shaken beliefs in determinism, unlimited progress, freedom, and happiness through reason, the superiority of western civilisation.

CHAPTER TWO

About society, groups, and community

We cannot discuss Freudian culture and society without situating them within their *natural* and *metapsychological* setting, reality and the external world, terms Freud frequently used that suggest ideas of social and cultural reality, but also sometimes *nature* or *material reality*, which is, as it happens, quite humanised. For him, it was therefore a matter of a different way of evoking this omnipresence and omnipotence that society and its culture—sources and places of "real external necessity", of the "power of the present", of constraints, exigencies, and "frustration of satisfaction", but also of instinctual satisfaction and of actions aiming, in particular, at adaptations, modifications, even at control and at sought-after satisfaction—represent for all human beings from the very beginning of their existence, then throughout the course of their lives. Let me also point to some significant pairs of opposites (psychic reality–actual reality; reality–motility; reality–thought; reality–phantasy, for example) that Freud introduced in reference to reality and the external world and inform us about the diverse conflicting and dialectical psychic relationships every individual establishes with them.

Reality and the external world

In "The neuro-psychoses of defence" (Freud, 1894a), Freud began introducing the expressions "reality", "piece of reality", "ego's detachment from reality" or from a piece of reality, corresponding to an irreconcilable representation arising in psychosis. Then, in his *Project for a Scientific Psychology* (Freud, 1895a), it is the expression "external world" that occurs upon numerous occasions as consisting of "powerful masses which are in violent motion and which transmit their motion". It is, in fact, "the origin of all major quantities of energy" (Freud, 1895d, p. 304), therefore of forms of excitation that the psychic apparatus will have to bring under control, in particular, by rejecting them. So, this very present external world is connected with perceptions and representations, notions of quantity and of quality.

At a very early point, this external world or this reality is considered a source of "frustration of satisfaction" and "actions" experienced in infancy. In fact, pathogenic or not, this "frustration" is doubly correlated with what is outside, and, more specifically with "limitations imposed by civilization" deriving from "demands of civilization" concerning access to satisfaction of the need for love by a "real object in the external world". These relationships are clearly defined in "Types of onset of neurosis" (1912c).

With "Short account of psycho-analysis" (1924f), let us look at the role of reality in "human cultural development", meaning in the fields, both individual and collective, of *Kulturarbeit*:

> the main motive force towards the cultural development of man has been the real external exigency, which has withheld from him the easy satisfaction of his natural needs and exposed him to immense dangers. The external frustration drove him into a struggle with reality, which ended partly in adaptation to it and partly in control over it; but it also drove him to working and living in common with those of his kind, and this already involved a renunciation of a number of instinctual impulses which could not be satisfied socially. (Freud, 1924f, p. 207)

In *Inhibitions, Symptoms and Anxiety* (Freud, 1926d), Freud clarified for us the ontogenetic significance—of a biological nature—of the influence of the external world on the small human child, more uncompleted than most animals, long in a state of very prolonged helplessness and dependency, instituting therefore its first situations of danger and creating its need to be loved, and the development of its ego, subject at an early stage to two concomitant sources of pressure, that of premature contact with the external world and those linked to the demands of sexuality.

Finally, in *Civilization and Its Discontents* (Freud, 1930a), Freud gave us one of his depictions of the external world as threatening, feared, from which one must defend oneself by turning away from it. Human suffering also comes from this external world, of which one can make oneself independent by seeking out one's own forms of gratification in internal psychic processes, by fantasising for example, just as when, represented by nature and its inexorable forces, recourse to technology guided by science makes it possible to subject it to the human will.

Nature

It is part of "reality", of the "external world", just as is society, the human community, groups, culture.

Still idolised for its innocence and beneficial qualities, by the end of the eighteenth century, nature had become a hostile, awe-inspiring force that human beings had to tame and dominate for their safety. From being mysterious and ethical, nature transformed itself into a force of production and capital to be made productive. Let us remember that the nineteenth century would witness the triumph of "materialistic naturalism", in which nature ultimately appeared as an external force to conquer and tame through efficacious human action and technology. This was a view and a project that Freud shared, as we are going to discover.

In Freudian writings, nature is also encountered in related forms such as science of nature, philosophy of nature, myth of nature, but also as suggesting constraint and domination, not to mention human nature or "what was originally animal in our nature" (Freud, 1910a, p. 54). An analogy can, moreover, be observed between the necessary control of the forces of nature and the necessary "taming" and "remoulding" of instincts, therefore, of the animal nature of human beings. *Kulturarbeit* and psychic work, as well as psychoanalytic work, actually display this analogy: the need for mastery and transformation of human and non-human nature in the service of what is human and of protecting it. This is expressed in an exemplary fashion by the definition of civilisation given in "The resistances to psycho-analysis", for which "Human civilization rests on two pillars, one of which is the control of the forces of nature and the other the restriction of our instincts" (Freud, 1925e, p. 219). Apart from this necessary control of the forces of nature, for the human community it is a matter of extracting "its wealth for the satisfaction of human needs" (Freud, 1927c, p. 6).

It is in *The Future of an Illusion* (Freud, 1927c) that Freud presents the *nature–culture* conflict, therefore, the very essence of culture which, according to him, would consist in protecting and preserving humanity from the dangers of nature, thus making the organisation of social life possible and necessary. He wrote,

> But how ungrateful, how short-sighted after all, to strive for the abolition of civilization! What would then remain would be a state of nature, and that would be far harder to bear. It is true that nature would not demand any restrictions of instinct from us, she would let us do as we liked; but she has her own particularly effective method of restricting us. She destroys us—coldly, cruelly, relentlessly, as it seems to us, and possibly through the very things that occasioned our satisfaction. It was precisely because of these dangers with which nature threatens us that we came together and created civilization, which is also, among other things, intended to make our communal life possible. *For the principal task of civilization, its actual* raison d'être, *is to defend us against nature.* (Freud, 1927c, p. 15, my emphasis)

However, also inquiring into the amount of happiness gained by human beings, Freud observed that they have not become happier due to this and found himself led to conclude that "power over nature is not the only precondition of human happiness, just as it is not the only goal of cultural endeavour" (Freud, 1927c, p. 88). In addition, through its use in the service of aggressive and destructive desires, technological progress made in controlling the forces of nature also has a harmful impact on social relationships between ethnic groups, nations—something that is also a reference to the "indomitableness of human nature" and the difficulties that it holds in store for any social community.

Introduction to the Freudian conception of society

Of course, I differentiate between society and culture, even though Freud rather frequently used those terms interchangeably, probably out of negligence, just as he also did with the terms of community and of group. What he says throughout his work is particularly rich and constitutes part of his personal socio-anthropology, elaborated independently of the writings of the founding fathers of those two fields, who were, however, his contemporaries. I am thinking, for example, of Emile Durkheim, and Max Weber, for sociology, and of Edward Burnett Tylor, James G. Frazer, Lewis Henry Morgan, and Franz Boas, for anthropology. This is why I shall devote a chapter to them.

Translation of key terms

Sozietät = society
Sozial = social
Gemeinschaft = community
Masse = group
Menge = crowd
Gruppe = group
Kollektiv = collective.

The relationship that Freud established between society and culture is often not clear. At best, it is a matter of a relationship between container and content. At worst, he uses the terms synonymously.

Community

The term *community* and the diverse ways in which it is used is particularly interesting to situate: human community; social community; cultural community, so important for civilisation; work community; and community of interest. As Freud said, "we can quite well imagine a cultural community consisting of double individuals like this, who libidinally satisfied in themselves, are connected with one another through the bonds of common work and common interests" (Freud, 1930a, p. 108). One also speaks of community bonds, feelings of community, attachment to a community, member of a community, insertion in or adaptation to a human community.

A question arises as to the sources of his uses of the word. Indeed, Ferdinand Tönnies, one of the German sociologists who was a contemporary of Freud, but also of Max Weber and of Georg Simmel, elaborated one of the best known typologies of forms of social organisation in the field of sociology (Tönnies, 1887). It was based on the distinction between community (*Gemeinschaft*) and society (*Gesellschaft*), which is itself based on another type of contrast, the psychological one between organic or primal will and that of will that is autonomous or built on detachment. Thus, the *Gemeinschaft* would participate in organic life, referring to familial bonds, while the *Gesellschaft* would participate in mechanical construction and contractual development involving individuals who are relatively independent from one another. It is, in fact, the interaction between these two types that proves to be of heuristic value according to contemporary sociologists. And, this very interaction seems to me to be found in the idea of community Freud used.

He also discussed the existence of a pathology of civilised communities and a possible diagnosis of "community neuroses" in *Civilization and Its Discontents* (Freud, 1930a), but also in his introduction to his book with William C. Bullitt, *Thomas Woodrow Wilson, Twenty-eighth President of the United States*, of which the following passage is particularly evocative,

> An increasingly delicate technique of diagnosis has shown us all sorts of neuroses where we least expected to find them; so that the statement is almost justified that neurotic symptoms and inhibitions have to a certain extent become common to all civilized beings. (Bullitt, 1966, p. xv)

Groups

Taking *Group Psychology and the Analysis of the Ego* (Freud, 1921c) as my point of departure, I am going to explore some of Freud's ideas about the notion of "groups" and their psychology that are integral parts of both his psychoanalytic sociology and his social psychology.

Groups display diversity, the types of which vary as a function of their number, their morphology, their organisation. Among them, Freud differentiated between leaderless groups and those with leaders. In particular, he chose two "artificial groups" displaying certain analogies: the Church and the Army. By "artificial", he meant that "a certain external force is employed to prevent them from disintegrating and to check alterations in their structure" (Freud, 1921c, p. 93).

Among those groups with leaders, it is appropriate to consider the possible substitution of an actual leader by a leading idea, common leanings, or a desire that all the participants share or to which they subscribe, which would be secondarily embodied in the person of a leader. The diverse interrelationships between the idea and the leader would be something to investigate.

According to Freud, "from the start individual psychology . . . is at the same time social psychology" (Freud, 1921c, p. 69) and pre-supposes, but also authorises, the psychoanalytic investigation of a psychology of groups. What is this group psychology?

> Group psychology is therefore concerned with the individual man as a member of a race, of a nation, of a caste, of a profession, of an insti-tution, or as a component part of a crowd of people who have been organized into a group at some particular time for some definite purpose. (Freud, 1921c, p. 70)

It is therefore only a matter of the individual and his or her social relationships within a group, and not of the group as an entity in terms of its specific functioning.

Prior to that, he had considered the "principal phenomenon of group psychology" to be an increase of affect and of inhibition of the intellect, then the lack of individual freedom in the primitive group. These phenomena are oriented towards an assimilation of other in-dividuals of the group, which needs and requires giving up the expressions of their own inclinations.

To shed light on group psychology, he proposed resorting to the concept of libido derived from the psychology of psychoneuroses and, in so doing, he proceeded to a *conceptual transfer* from the indi-vidual domain towards the collective domain. This group is clearly unified by the power of Eros, which tends towards union and harmony in the world.

He discussed the "group mind" that he was therefore going to explore with this concept of libido and "emotional ties" constitutive of the group and of its "mind", particularly within the artificial groups the Church and the Army. In them, the illusion prevails that a supreme leader is there—Christ in the Catholic Church, in the armed forces, the commander-in-chief—who loves all the individuals of the group with an equal love. Each individual is tied libidinally, on the one hand, to the leader (Christ, commander-in-chief), and, on the other hand, to the individuals making up the group. How do these two ties relate to one another? Are they of the same nature? Do they have the same value?

Freud also envisaged the situation in which the leader or the idea, the institution, could become "negative", arousing then hostility toward them, but also unifying libidinal ties within the group in question.

If group formation requires the establishment of libidinal ties among its members, remembering that *love has acted as a factor in culture*, or more precisely as a factor in creating social bonds and social feeling, both in the individual and in evolution, it implies some preconditions and consequences for each one of them: limitation of their narcissism, therefore of their peculiarities and differences, in favour of their similarities and of object-love, which could only inhibit their hostility born of narcissistic self-affirmation intolerant of the slightest deviation and the slightest difference. Thus, in the group, the individuals will behave as if they were alike and tolerate the attenuated distinctiveness of the others. Nevertheless, according to Freud, the essence of this group formation implies the existence of libidinal ties of a new sort, for which he appealed to the concept of identification that, from then on, would render the notion of social instinct useless—insufficiently precise, no doubt.

In so doing, Freud succeeded in being able to elucidate the libidinal structure of a group with a leader composed of a certain number of individuals by differentiating the ego from the ego ideal and the double kind of tie thus made possible: identification and the putting of the object in the place of the ego ideal. They have then put a single object (the leader, the idea) in the place of their ego ideal and have consequently identified with one another in their ego. In addition, Freud observed that each individual participates in the constitution of "many groups" to which he or she is bound through identification and that he or she even creates his or her ego ideal in accordance with quite diverse models, something that led him to consider that "each individual therefore has a share in numerous group-minds—those of his race, of his creed, of his nationality, etc.—and he can also raise himself above them to the extent of having a scrap of independence and originality" (Freud, 1921c, p. 129), something that, astonishingly, connects up with the Durkheimian idea that every individual belongs to several "collective consciousnesses".

Nevertheless, Freud sensed the need to complete his "libidinal formula" further by adding the prevalent participation of aim-inhibited impulsions, which cannot be entirely satisfied, but whose great functional advantage over directly sexual instincts consists in the creation of permanent ties.

In addition, he tells us that within these groups composed of men and women, the difference between sexes plays no role and, thus, the libido ensuring the cohesion does not differ from sex to sex. Finally, neurosis, which makes people asocial, has a "disintegrating effect" upon the group comparable to that of being in love.

Freud ultimately came to a "complete libidinal formula" for a group having a leader that could account for one of the essential aspects of its "mind". *It was based, on the one hand, on aim-inhibited libidinal ties and on identifications among members made possible by the same relation to the object-leader, and, on the other hand, on the replacement of each one's ego ideal by that object-leader.*

Described in this manner, this sort of group, characterised by the image of an "individual of superior strength among a troop of equal companions" suggested to Freud a regressive representation of the primal horde, but also its revival, therefore a phylogenetic bond, with the double psychology correlative to it: that of individuals of the group bound by identifications and aim-inhibited sexual instincts, having a passion for authority and thirsty to obey; and that of the feared, all-powerful, free father, representing the group ideal that dominates the ego in place of the individuals' ego ideal. Freud considered that, just as "primitive man survives potentially in every individual, so the primal horde may arise once more out of any random collection" (Freud, 1921c, p. 123).

Society

Lexical aspects of Freudian society

Society, human society, society of civilisation

Here are some terms and expressions found from the origins of society up to its evolution and progress.

> Origin of society; primal state of society; "human beings' primal social state"; the human horde dominated, without restriction, by

a strong male as the primal form of human society; foundation of society.

Social order; social organisation; social classes and strata; the "upper affluent strata of society" and "large lower classes"; social configurations; social differences; social inequality. Social systems; social institutions.

Social relations; social instincts; social feelings.

Social demands; cultural demands of society: "the ethical restrictions demanded by society" (Freud, 1916–1917, p. 432); "Restriction of the individual's aggressiveness is the first and perhaps the severest sacrifice which society demands of him" (Freud, 1933a, Lecture XXXII, p. 110); social commandments; social constraint; social injunction; authority of society; social authority; "ideal set up by society" (Freud, 1915–1916, p. 205).

Social adaptation: finding one's "place in a society which is full of other individuals making equally strong demands" (Freud, 1908e, p, 147).

Social training; society's educational tasks: "society must take as one of its most important educative tasks to tame and restrict the sexual instinct when it breaks out as an urge to reproduction, and to subject it to an individual will which is identical with the bidding of society" (Freud, 1916–1917, p, 311).

The suggestion of society; tolerance of society.

The motives of human society.

The motive of human society is in the last resort an economic one; since it does not possess enough provisions to keep its members alive unless they work, it must restrict the number of its members and divert their energies from sexual activity to work. It is faced, in short, by the eternal, primaeval exigencies of life, which are with us to this day (Freud, 1916–1917, p. 312).

The development of society; the evolution of society; "The whole progress of society rests upon the opposition between successive generations" (Freud, 1909c, p. 237).

Let us look more particularly at certain sectors of society studied by Freud: the social institutions, notions of social instincts and social feelings, but also that of social anxiety.

Social institutions

In the course of reading Freud's work, one spots terminological fluctuations, notably when it is a case of institutions, which are sometimes social, sometimes cultural, even human. The list of institutions itself fluctuates. However, the social or civic order, even social organisation, religion, morals or ethics, and law figure there fairly regularly. I shall expand upon them in the part devoted to culture and its main contents.

In *Totem and Taboo* (Freud, 1912–1913), then in "The claims of psycho-analysis to scientific interest" (Freud, 1913j), based on the new understanding of neuroses and their paradigm, Freud provided an explanation of the existence and process of forming institutions, both of them a matter of instinctual conflicts and constituting compromise solutions to the problem of compensation of wishes— neuroses being individual and asocial, institutions being social, therefore accomplished collectively, collective products of *Kulturarbeit*. Social institutions are considered to be mankind's greatest assets and psychoanalysis has revealed their instinctual and "animal" origin. In addition, in " 'Civilized' sexual morality and modern nervous illness", Freud emphasised their close correlation and "the difficulty of altering any part without regard for the whole" (Freud, 1908d, p. 196), which indicates to us their "systemic" nature, but he would not formulate this in that way. According to the hypothesis put forward in *Totem and Taboo*,

> they were acquired phylogenetically out of the "father-complex": religion and moral restraint through the process of mastering the Œdipus complex itself, and social feeling through the obligation for overcoming the rivalry that remained between the members of the younger generation. (Freud, 1923b, p. 37)

In 1921, in "Group psychology and the analysis of the ego", these institutions of society come into being as *crystallisations* of the unity and stability of groups "in which mankind pass their lives". It is, in fact, a matter of every society's creating a common body for itself, a place of unity and cohesion of a human community. At the same time, Freud indicated to us that these stable groups, therefore, societies, are "containers of life" for their members: "those stable groups or associations *in which* mankind pass their lives, and which are *embodied* in the institutions of society" (Freud, 1921c, p. 83, my emphasis).

Later on, in 1924, he explains that, having come into being simultaneously in the "prehistoric times of humanity", they represent "a third and extremely serious part of human intellectual activity", which "has as its fundamental aim enabling the individual to master his Oedipus complex and to divert his libido from its infantile attachments into the social ones that are ultimately desired" (Freud, 1924f, p. 208).

Moreover, this activity of the human mind is one of the forms of expression of the "group mind" capable of other mental creations, "as is shown above all by language itself, as well as by folk-song, folklore and the like" (Freud, 1921c, p. 83).

Social instincts and social feelings

The notion of *social instinct* appears for the first time in 1911 in "Psycho-analytic notes on an autobiographical account of a case of paranoia" (Freud, 1911c) preceded by the mention "altruistic impulses" associated with morality in children, by nature egoistic, in *The Interpretation of Dreams* (Freud, 1900a, p. 250). It would only be abandoned after 1926, and during this fifteen year period, social instincts and social feelings would exist side by side.

Right from the beginning, Freud defined them as essentially homosexual aim-inhibited erotic instincts that combine with ego instincts, therefore, with selfishness. Consequently, it is not a matter of primal instincts that "do not admit of further dissection", as he would explain in "Instincts and their vicissitudes" (Freud, 1915c, p. 124).

Here is the seminal text:

> After the choice of heterosexual object-choice has been reached, the homosexual tendencies are not, as might be supposed, done away with or brought to a stop; they are merely deflected from their sexual aim and applied to fresh uses. They now combine with portions of the ego instincts and, as "attached" components, help to constitute the *social instincts*, thus contributing an erotic factor to friendship and to the love of mankind in general. How large a contribution is, in fact, derived from erotic sources (with the sexual aim inhibited) could scarcely be guessed from the normal social relations of mankind. But it is not irrelevant to note that it is precisely manifest homosexuals, and among them again precisely those that set themselves against an indulgence in sensual acts, who are distinguished by taking a

particularly active share in the general interests of humanity—interests which have themselves sprung from a sublimation of erotic instincts. (Freud, 1911c, p. 61)

Then in *Totem and Taboo* (Freud, 1912–1913), he took up the above definition again, without bringing up the homosexual nature of the erotic component, but brings up the creation of those "wholes of a special kind" upon which cultural formations are based, unlike neurotic formations, by nature asocial, based essentially upon instinctual forces that are sexual in origin. Found there are also "social feelings" and "social fraternal feelings":

For a long time afterwards, the *social fraternal feelings*, which were the basis of this whole transformation, continued to exercise a profound influence on the development of society. They found expression in the sanctification of the blood tie, in the emphasis upon the solidarity of all life within the same clan. (Freud, 1912–1913, p. 146)

Later, in "Thoughts for the times on war and death", Freud looked at the creation of social instincts, that is to say the transformation, the remodelling or change of "bad", egoistic, trends into altruistic ones by the admixture of erotic elements, originating in an "susceptibility to culture"—made up of an innate part as a form of organisation inherited from the cultural history of one's ancestors, and a part acquired in the course of life itself—and as one of the aims of *Kulturarbeit*, work of civilisation, at work in every individual, but also to be connected to its phylogenetic dimension. This remodelling instinct is the product of two factors, one internal, consisting in an admixture of erotism, the other external, the force exercised by one's upbringing, then the influences of civilisation (Freud, 1915b, pp. 282–283).

In *A Phylogenetic Fantasy, Overview of the Transference Neuroses* (Freud, 1912), Freud presented the "social feelings" from a phylogenetic perspective—corresponding to the clan of brothers born of a sublimation of homosexuality—that have become a component of mankind's legacy and one of the foundations of every society.

After having looked at their phylogenesis, in *Totem and Taboo*, and then in "Thoughts for the times on war and death", Freud inquired into their ontogenesis in "Group psychology and the analysis of the ego". He observed their absence at the onset of early childhood and analysed the conditions of their emergence as well as the processes at work. In fact, the inevitable presence among siblings of intense jealousy and hostility in connection with the children's relationships with their parents or with the "mother-complex" would be subject— owing to the influence of the children's upbringing and out of the impossibility of satisfaction—to repression, then to a change of feelings through reactive formation, in such a way that rival siblings would become the first objects of homosexual love—which is the "the complete contrast to the development of persecutory paranoia in which the person who has before been loved becomes the hated persecutor, whereas here the hated rivals are transformed into love-objects" (Freud, 1921c, pp. 230–232).

At a later point, the introduction of the identification component enabled him to connect the two processes, that of reactive formation to attitudes of hostile rivalry and that of identifying with others on the basis of a "common bond of affection", with an ego ideal figure. But, based on his observations of "slightly homosexual" persons, he found that identification becomes a substitute for a choice of object of affection that took over from the hostile attitude of rivalry. These connections between homosexuality and "social sensitivity" were going to shed light on certain processes at work, notably on the transformation of the hostile-rival attitude toward the object into an affectionate investment, in the form of an object-choice or of an identification. He then determined that those social feelings proceed from *sublimations* of homosexual attitudes towards objects.

Finally, inquiring into the possible existence of a direct transformation of hate into love in homosexuality in "The ego and the id" (Freud, 1923b), through analytic investigation of the processes involved in the "change of paranoia", Freud, in fact, discovered an ambivalent attitude present right from the onset. Indeed, there occurs a displacement of investment of energy being withdrawn from the hostile rivalry that has no prospect of satisfaction and, for economic reasons, is added to the erotic impulse, therefore, to the loving attitude, which offers greater such prospects.

After 1926, we no longer encounter these notions of social instincts and social feelings, in particular, neither in *The Future of an Illusion*, nor in *Civilization and Its Discontents*. Rather we find that of asocial instincts that religion contributes and endeavours to tame.

Social anxiety

From the beginning, social anxiety referred to feelings of reproach linked to sexual behaviour engaged in by the child and the fear of being reprimanded by society. Then, it very rapidly became associated with a sense of guilt, or "conscience anxiety", originally anxiety about being punished by one's parents by loss of their love and later on by *others*, members of the social community. In "Thoughts for the times on war and death" (Freud, 1915b), Freud reminded us that our conscience originates in "social anxiety". Then, in "Group psychology and the analysis of the ego" (Freud, 1921c), social anxiety constituted its essence. Curiously, with the development of superego, meaning the "depersonalization of the parental agency", but whose essence remains the parental introjected agency, castration anxiety is then transformed into "undefined moral or social anxiety" (Freud, 1926d, p. 139). The latter thus preserves its quality of essence of the conscience and acquires a new, more up-to-date property. Two temporalities come together.

Finally, in *Civilization and Its Discontents* (Freud, 1930a), Freud established a correlation between evil, the sense of guilt, and social anxiety based on the threat of the loss of one's parents' love, then of the social community.

Psychoanalysis in society

In several texts, *Introductory Lectures on Psycho-Analysis Part III* (1916–1917) and "The resistances to psycho-analysis" (Freud, 1925e) in particular, Freud discussed the social and cultural situation of psychoanalysis *banned* by the bourgeois social order as being a "danger to society" and "hostile to civilization" owing to its critical attitude and the perception of the threatening nature of the therapeutic repercussions of practising it. Indeed, by according great significance to sexual instincts in psychic life, notably in producing neuroses, it was endeavouring to show that these very sexual components, which may be diverted from their immediate aims and lead to others, constitute the "the most important contributions to the cultural achievements of the individual and of society", among which figure art, religion, and the social order, something that appeared to involve a "degradation of the highest cultural values" (Freud, 1925e, p. 218).

Freud also maintained that psychoanalysis is observant and critical, but not reformative with regard to society, the raising of its children, and the moral demands imposed upon its members—notably those linked to conventional sexual morality—who see themselves forced to live beyond their capabilities without any compensation for the sacrifices required and endangering their psychic equilibrium, something that produces a *state of cultural hypocrisy* and keeps it going. It thus exposes weaknesses of that system.

Let us first of all look at some of his reflections on education and the role that psychoanalysis could play:

> Unless this problem is entirely insoluble, an optimum must be discovered which will enable education to achieve the most and damage the least. It will therefore be a matter of deciding how much to forbid, at what times and by what means. And in addition we have to take into account that the objects of our educational influence have very different innate constitutional dispositions, so that it is quite impossible that the same educational procedure can be equally good for all children. A moment's reflection tells us that hitherto education has fulfilled its task very badly and has done children great damage. (Freud, 1933a, Lecture XXXIV, p. 149)

So, where do matters stand, for example, regarding the usual practice of hiding sexual matters from children, and must one rather "enlighten" them somewhat in this bourgeois society of the beginning of the twentieth century? In his text "The sexual enlightenment of children" (Freud, 1907c), contemporaneous with two others, fairly closely related ones "On the sexual theories of children" (Freud, 1908c) and " 'Civilized' sexual morality and modern nervous illness" (Freud, 1908d), Freud then pondered a number of reasons for forbidding children any opportunity to satisfy their curiosity.

However, for Freud, education also concerns adults belonging to the social category of "leaders" or the "upper class" in a society organised, according to him, in terms of a split imputable to human inequality, part of which is innate, between "dependent subjects" imbued with a need for authority, constituting the vast majority and having a "low level of morality", and the stratum of people "with independent minds, not open to intimidation and eager in the pursuit of truth, whose business it would be to give direction to the dependent masses" (Freud, 1933b, p. 212).

In addition, if psychoanalysis does not aim to reform, it does nevertheless propose to modify to a certain extent. It was at this point that Freud presented, on the one hand, the benefits of an *education that was psychoanalytically oriented* but not in the service of the demands of the bourgeois social order, and on the other hand, the *after-education* that psychoanalytic treatment might represent for his patients.

But what would a psychoanalytically oriented education involve and what goals might it be expected to fulfil? An answer is provided in his commentary on the works of Reverend Pfister:

> Education should scrupulously refrain from burying these precious springs of action and should restrict itself to encouraging the processes by which these energies are led along safe paths. Whatever we expect in the way of prophylaxis against neurosis in the individual lies in the hands of a psychoanalytically enlightened education. (Freud, 1913j, p. 190)

What exactly is psychoanalytic after-education?

In number of texts, Freud envisages this "after-education" of the neurotic adult "as a corrective to his education as a child" (Freud, 1926f, p. 268), therefore, different from the education of children, uncompleted beings and not yet neurotic. More particularly, "The question of lay analysis" speaks of the education of the ego described in the following fashion:

> We try to restore the ego, to free it from its restrictions, and to give it back the command over the id which it has lost owing to its early repressions. It is for this one purpose that we carry out analysis, our whole technique is directed to this aim . . . . By encouraging the patient to disregard his resistances to telling us these things, we are educating his ego to overcome its inclination towards attempts at flight and to tolerate an approach to what is repressed. (Freud, 1926e, p. 205)

However, this after-education is only possible if the patient places the analyst in the place of his or her father (or his or her mother), thus giving the analyst,

> the power which his super-ego exercises over his ego, since his parents were, as we know, the origin of his super-ego. The new super-ego now has an opportunity for a sort of *after-education* of the neurotic; it can

correct mistakes for which his parents were responsible in educating
him. But at this point a warning must be given against misusing this
new influence. (Freud, 1940a, p. 175)

Consequently, this psychoanalytic after-education provides an
opportunity to lessen the severity of the repressive instinct, to autho-
rise certain instincts to enjoy a greater measure of satisfaction, to
develop sublimational capacities, but also to give more room to truth-
fulness because psychoanalysis educates one to be true to oneself. In
addition, Freud acknowledges that psychoanalytic treatment does not
place itself in the service of "conventional morality" or "socially
accepted good morals". As he wrote, "what it has given to the individual, it will have taken from the community" (Freud, 1916–1917,
p. 337). Thus, once the treatment of patients has come to an end,
having become independent from then on, "they decide on their own
judgement in favour of a midway position between living a full life
and absolute asceticism". They are then "permanently defended
against the danger of immorality", even though their "standard of
morality may differ from that which is customary in society" (Freud,
1916–1917, p. 434).

Besides questions about education and the social role played by
psychoanalysis, let us take a look at Freud's ideas about the institution
of bourgeois marriage and its harmful effects on both sexes as well as
on their progeny discussed in 1908 in his " 'Civilized' sexual morality
and modern nervous illness".

Our "civilized sexual morality" not only requires abstinence before
marriage, but also restricts marital sexual life by imposing upon
married couples the necessity of contenting themselves, as a rule, with
a very small number of children. So, both marriage partners find
themselves brought back to the situation they were in prior to their
marriage and once again facing cultural requirements about the
mastery and sublimation of instincts (Freud, 1908d, pp. 193–194).
Based on this, Freud depicted for us a socially instituted sexual difference regarding the ways of dealing with this painful situation. For
men who have reached a more mature age,

Experience shows that they very frequently avail themselves of the
degree of sexual freedom which is allowed them—although only with
reluctance and under the veil of silence—by even the strictest sexual

code. The "double" sexual morality which is valid for men in our society is the plainest admission that society itself does not believe in the
possibility of enforcing the precepts which it itself has laid down.
(Freud, 1908d, p. 195)

As for women,

> who, as being the actual vehicle of the sexual interests of mankind,
> are only endowed in a small measure with the gift of sublimating
> their instincts and who, may find a sufficient substitute for the sexual
> object in an infant at the breast, do not find one in a growing child—
> experience shows, I repeat, that women, when they are subject to the
> disillusionments of marriage, fall ill with severe neuroses which
> permanently darken their lives. (Freud, 1908d, p. 195)

So, Freud considers that,

> the cure for nervous illness arising from marriage would be marital
> unfaithfulness. But the more strictly a woman has been brought up
> and the more sternly she has submitted to the demands of civilization,
> the more she is afraid of taking this way out; and in the conflict
> between her desires and her sense of duty, she once more seeks refuge
> in a neurosis. Nothing protects her as securely as an illness. (Freud,
> 1908d, p. 195)

What are some of the negative consequences of this situation
Freud identified?

If normal sexual life is suppressed by this morality, then there is a
rise in the frequency of what are known as perverted modes of relationships between the sexes, as well as an increase in homosexual
satisfaction. But that is not all. Indeed, he observed, in addition, the
repercussions of such a conjugal situation on the children of this traditional bourgeois couple—whose mother would be neurotic—in the
form of neurotic destinies with "powerful infantile impressions".
Finally, he described one of the modes of intergenerational transmission of nervous illness within his society:

> A neurotic wife who is unsatisfied by her husband is, as a mother, over-
> tender and over-anxious towards her child, on to whom she transfers
> her need for love; and she awakens it to sexual precocity. The bad rela-
> tions between its parents, moreover, excite its emotional life and cause
> it to feel love and hatred to an intense degree while it is still at a very

tender age. Its strict upbringing, which tolerates no activity of the sexual life that has been aroused so early, lends support to the suppressing force and this conflict at such an age contains everything necessary for bringing about lifelong nervous illness. (Freud, 1908d, p. 202)

I shall leave matters here for the question of society and shall now discuss Freudian culture.

CHAPTER THREE

Freudian culture

Thoughts on the genealogy of Freudian Kultur

T he German feminine noun *die Kultur* is derived from the Latin word *cultura*, which comes from the verb *colere* (*colui, cultus*), cultivate, work the soil, and by extension, to inhabit, care for. What is the source of *Kultur* in Freud, and how did he use it? To answer that question, I must clarify some points:

- The cultural, social, and historical context in which Freud's thought evolved was that of the liberal *moyenne bourgeoisie* of Viennese society of the latter half of the nineteenth century and the beginning of the twentieth, more particularly that of physicians, scholars, and academics influenced by German thought and its intellectuals for whom the notion of *Kultur* had a quite specific meaning different from that of the German and Austrian nobility, as well as from that of the foreign nobility, French and English in particular. With the sociologist Norbert Elias (Elias, 1939), we are going to discover that specific meaning.
- There is the *Kultur* of ordinary, everyday language, and that of scholars, specialists in the nascent social sciences, anthropology

and sociology. Might Freud have borrowed the term from every-day language or from that of the human sciences? Very probably from everyday language, I contend.

- The problem of the distinction between culture and civilisation arises here as well.

The German notion of Kultur

According to Norbert Elias (Elias, 1939), the German notion *Kultur* is to be understood in terms of its conflicting relationship with that of *Zivilization*, which is connected with the historical conflict between the nobility and the bourgeoisie. It was the creation of German intellectuals belonging to the *moyenne bourgeoisie* in the eighteenth century, in opposition to the court society influenced by the French aristocracy and its civilisation, dominant in European courts, but it was also as part of a search for characteristics and values of "German national" identity that was inherent in the difficulties of political and territorial unification. *Kultur* essentially designates religious, artistic, and intellectual "achievements", thus tending to establish a fairly clear dividing line with the social, economic, and political deeds typifying groups and national differences.

According to Elias, it was owing to this role in establishing boundary lines that it was able to acquire significance well beyond its original context and to extend beyond the German linguistic zone into the fields of ethnology and anthropology, for example. Consider Franz Boas, of German origin, the founder of American anthropology, characterised by its "culturalistic" approach. However, that "original context" is that of a people which, in comparison to other western peoples, was very late in achieving political unification and consolidation.

The French notion of civilisation

This German *Kultur* stands in contrast to *Zivilization*, which would for Germans above all represent the outer side of human beings, the surface of human existence.

While for the French and the English, it referred to two realities. On the one hand, it referred to the social, ethical, technological, religious, economic, and political deeds that are objects of national pride, and, on the other hand, to progress made by the West and humanity in general.

Elias, in fact, teaches us that this is a French notion that, just like the German notion of *Kultur*, grew out of opposition by intellectuals of the *moyenne bourgeoisie* of the second half of the eighteenth century. The differences in the process of formation, of function, and meaning between the French concept and the corresponding German concept reflect differences in the situation and behaviour of the middle classes in the two countries.

This notion is first found in French literature at the beginning of the second half of the eighteenth century in the work of the elder Mirabeau, deriving at that time from a broadening of the meaning of the verb "to civilize". Indeed, the elder Mirabeau and the intellectuals drew *civilisation* as the general characteristic of society from the ideals of the aristocracy or court society—characterised by the image of civilised, honest, and cultivated persons, but also by politeness and good manners—by which this dominant European stratum of society sought to set itself apart and display its sense of superiority over other social strata deemed socially less developed.

As a consequence, this notion of civilisation contains two different ideas.

As a general term, it stands in contrast to another stage in the evolution of society, "barbarism". Court society had long been conscious of the progress made in this regard, which had found concrete expression at its level in terms such as "politeness" or "civility". But the population was not yet sufficiently civilised, the bourgeois reformers of the court maintained. Civilisation is not only a *state*; it is a *process* to be promoted. That was the new idea also expressed by the notion of "civilization". But this rising middle class, this reform movement, accorded broader meaning to the criteria making a society a civilised society. This civilising of the different sectors of society must go along with the refinement of mores and the domestic pacification of the country by the kings.

With the bourgeoisie's accession to positions of power in the nation, this notion also became *the expression of national feeling*. At the end of the century, the word "civilization", designating a slow, evolving process originating in reformist ideas, became fashionable, known around the world, and served as a justification for France's expansionist and colonising inclinations.

What about culture and civilisation in the social sciences in Freud's time?

These notions testify to the advent of social and cultural anthropology and stemmed from an evolution, a transition, from the notion of *race* associated with the anthropology of the surgeon and anthropologist Paul Broca (1824–1880).

He was, in fact, the first to define the purpose of anthropology as synthetic knowledge principally conceived of as the particular description and determination of the races, the study of their similarities and dissimilarities from the point of view of intellectual and social state (Broca, 1871). Based on this assumption, he and his disciples founded the field of craniology, which used measurements of the volume of craniums to establish a close correlation between inborn physical differences and norms, the behaviour of human groups and the socio-economic differences characterising them. Correlations of that kind were to inspire the racialist theories predominant in the nineteenth century, with the notion of race as the "key" concept, thus naturalising socio-cultural accomplishments. The fundamental criticism of the notion of "race" came from the French school of sociology, and Emile Durkheim and Marcel Mauss would appeal to the word "civilization" to characterise the sociological study of human accomplishments. They provided a definition of it that underscored instead its universality embodied in all societies in their institutions, structures, values, and symbols. In parallel fashion, in Great Britain, Edward Burnett Tylor elaborated the notion of "culture" along the same lines, taking it from the German concept *Kultur*, in contrast to the tradition of "erudite culture", then broadened to include human accomplishments as a whole and extended to humanity as a whole as something universally given, an expression of the unity of the human spirit.

For my part, I have observed that Freud used *Kultur* indiscriminately to designate both culture and civilisation.

Culture, domain of expression and of projection of human intellectual activity

According to Freud, culture represents the field of expression and of accomplishments of "human intellectual activity", which he differentiated and subdivided into "three parts" in his "Short account of psycho-analysis" (Freud, 1924f), and which, as it happens, proceeds from one of the major psychical processes particularly highlighted in *Totem and Taboo*, normal projection.

These three "parts of human intellectual activity" (Freud, 1924f, pp. 207–208), in fact, correspond to the three sectors of his depiction of culture:

- The first is oriented towards a struggle with reality, adaptation and gaining control over the real external world, over nature, aiming at protecting and acquiring the necessities of life, thus driving people into working and living in common. It is curious to note that in 1924 Freud considered real external exigency to be the principal motive force behind human cultural development, while in 1930, in *Civilization and Its Discontents*, he would associate internal erotic urges in this.
- The second serves for the substitutive satisfaction of the repressed wishes, which from childhood live unsatisfied in the psyche of each person. Indeed, if sexual instincts commonly succumb to cultural suppression, a part of them can be sublimated, thus putting their energy at the disposal of cultural development, while another part remains in the form of unsatisfied wishes pressing for satisfaction of any kind, even distorted. Myths, creative writing, and art figure among those creations.
- A third part created the great institutions of religion, law, ethics, and all "forms of civic life", and "has as its fundamental aim the enabling of the individual to master his Oedipus complex and to divert his libido from its infantile attachments into the social ones that are ultimately desired" (Freud, 1924f, p. 208).

Chronological and terminological overview

It seems that the first mention of the word *"Kultur"* figured in the "Draft N. notes" added to Freud's May 31, 1897 letter to Fliess:

Definition of "Holiness": "Holiness" is something based on the fact that human beings, for the benefit of the larger community, have sacrificed a portion of their sexual liberty and their liberty to indulge in perversions. The horror of incest (something impious) is based on the fact that, as a result of community of sexual life (even in childhood) the members of a family hold together permanently and become incapable of contact with strangers. Thus incest is antisocial—civilization consists in this progressive renunciation. Contrariwise the "super-man". (Freud, 1892, p. 257)

He used the term "civilization" in "On the psychical mechanism of hysterical phenomena" writing,

But, as an English writer has wittily remarked, the man who first flung a word of abuse at his enemy instead of a spear was the founder of civilization. Thus words are substitutes for deeds and in some circumstances (e.g. in Confession) the only substitutes. (Freud, 1893h, p. 36)

And he also used it in 1896, regarding criticism of the ideas of George Miller Beard on neurasthenia. Curiously, he chose the word "civilization" (modern) and society, rather than the word "culture", which he would introduce in 1897 and, unlike the word "civilization", would never abandon—according to the facts provided in the new French translation of Freud's complete works edited by Jean Laplanche (Freud, 2010).

Kulturarbeit first appears in *The Interpretation of Dreams* (Freud, 1900a) where it is translated by "cultural activity".

Then we are going to find throughout his writings a number of terms and expressions exploring and qualifying diverse aspects of culture, on both the collective and the individual level, but also from the twofold, diachronic and synchronic, perspective. So it is, for example, with the expressions "cultural development" and human "cultural development" in " 'Civilized' sexual morality and modern nervous illness" (Freud, 1908d); "the individual capable of becoming a civilized and useful member of society" in "Analysis of a phobia in a five-year-old boy", (Freud, 1909b, p. 146); susceptibility to culture, cultural society (a quite odd combination), cultural and uncivilised behaviour, the notion of "cultural hypocrisy" in "Thoughts for the times on war and death" (Freud, 1915b). Based on the study of infantile neuroses, he points to "the absence of any aspirations towards remote cultural aims" in children in "From the history of an infantile neurosis" (Freud, 1918b, p. 9).

Moreover, pursuant to his *Three Essays on the Theory of Sexuality* (Freud, 1905d), in his *Introductory Lectures on Psycho-Analysis* (Parts I and II), he reaffirms the libidinal, instinctual foundations of culture "created under the pressure of the exigencies of life" with its "highest cultural, artistic and social creations of the human spirit". But these libidinal phenomena are also at work in the "causation of nervous and mental diseases" (Freud, 1915–1916, p. 22). In addition, a more specific type of relation between culture and society is put forth,

> in the case of every individual who is supposed to join in the work of civilization, there is a risk that his sexual instincts may refuse to be put to that use. Society believes that no greater threat to *its civilization* could arise than if the sexual instincts were to be liberated and returned to their original aims. For this reason society does not wish to be reminded of this precarious portion of its foundations. (Freud, 1915–1916, p. 23, my emphasis)

Later on, from 1916 to 1920, we find "the cultural aims of the ego's organisation" and once again "human cultural development" based on detaching and developing the human "animal archaic heritage", innate reservoir of instinctual forces.

From 1921 to 1923, Freud introduced the notion of "cultural suppression", in the wake of the exigencies, of the pressure of culture and obedience to culture. Then development towards culture, the "main motive force towards cultural development", with the analogy that would regularly be found between phylogenesis and ontogenesis.

Moreover, we find "love as a factor of culture", both in the individual and in the evolution of humanity, in the sense of "change of egoism into altruism", of holding narcissism in check.

In *New Introductory Lectures* (1933a), Freud also identifies the existence of "cultural demands of the individual" to which a "new social order" will have to "give a hearing". (Freud, 1933a, Lecture XXXV, p. 181)

In addition, the process of the development of culture, or cultural development, is comparable to an organic process. Finally, he introduces the existence of "psychological characteristics of civilization" (Freud, 1933b, p. 214).

However, it is in *The Future of an Illusion* that Freud offered his fullest definition of culture, which he would later pare down in *Civilization and Its Discontents* (Freud, 1930a):

> Human civilization, by which I mean all those respects in which human life has raised itself above its animal status and differs from the

life of beasts—and I scorn to distinguish between culture and civilization—presents, as we know, two aspects to the observer. It includes on
the one hand all the knowledge and capacity that men have acquired
in order to control the forces of nature and extract its wealth for the
satisfaction of human needs, and, on the other hand, all the regulations necessary in order to adjust the relations of men to one another
and especially the distribution of available wealth. The two trends of
civilization are not independent of each other. (Freud, 1927c, pp. 5–6)

Moreover, he presents there that other fundamental conflict, that
between culture and the individual, which would be taken up in a
different manner in the conflict between psychoanalysis and culture:

every individual is virtually an enemy of civilization, though civilization is supposed to be an object of universal human interest. It is
remarkable that, little as men are able to exist in isolation, they should
nevertheless feel as a heavy burden the sacrifices which civilization
expects of them in order to make a communal life possible. Thus civilization has to be defined against the individual, and its regulations,
institutions and commands are directed to that task. (Freud, 1927c, p. 6)

Indeed, bringing up certain "characteristic features", as well as
"regulations", "institutions", and "commands", but also "its tasks",
Freud would begin a description of certain aspects of culture, something I shall return to at a later point.

I would also like to point to the often conflicting relationships
suggested by Freud between: culture and society (society and its
culture); culture and nature; culture and the individual; culture and
sexuality; culture and differences between the sexes; culture and
neurosis; culture and psychoanalysis.

Instinctual foundations and the essence of culture

Freud considered that,

Historians of civilization appear to be at one in assuming that powerful components are acquired for every kind of cultural achievement by
this diversion of sexual instinctual forces from sexual aims and their
direction to new ones—a process, which deserves the name of "sublimation". To this we would add, accordingly, that the same process

plays a part in the development of the individual and we place its beginning in the period of sexual latency of childhood. (Freud, 1905d, p. 178)

The individual and collective process of sublimation therefore
asserts itself as a participant in the constitution of culture just as other
processes do. And on the individual level, it contributes to the cultural
development of children, and therefore to their socialisation.

In 1925, in "The resistances to psycho-analysis", Freud added that
these same sexual components constitute "the most important contributions to the cultural achievements of the individual and of society"
(Freud, 1925e, p. 218). In addition, these sublimated, or restrained,
aim-inhibited, even repressed, instinctual components, object of
renunciation, of sacrifices and remodelling, represent "the mental
assets of civilization", Freud maintained in *The Future of an Illusion*
(Freud, 1927c, p. 10). He, nevertheless, associated other components
with this that we shall look at later on. In *Civilization and Its
Discontents*, he confirms that culture obeys

> the laws of economic necessity, since a large amount of the psychical
> energy which it uses for its own purposes has to be withdrawn from
> sexuality. In this respect civilization behaves toward sexuality as a
> people or stratum of its population does which has subjected another
> one to its exploitation. (Freud, 1930a, p. 104)

Culture is at the same time a source of protection against the
dangers of nature, but also a source of many kinds of suffering, such
as those due to the instinctual renunciation required of each one of its
participants. According to Freud, the true foundation of the existence
of culture, becomes confused with its principal task. We have gathered
together to protect ourselves from the threatening dangers of nature
and to control it in order to procure the necessities of life for ourselves.
It is therefore a matter of preserving mankind in face of the "superior
power of nature", something that brought him to write in *Civilization
and Its Discontents*,

> We recognize as cultural all activities and resources which are useful
> to men for making the earth serviceable to them, for protecting them
> against the violence of the forces of nature, and so on. As regards this
> side of civilization, there can be scarcely any doubt. If we go back far
> enough, we find that the first acts of civilization were the use of tools,

the gaining of control over fire and the construction of dwellings. Among these, the control over fire stands out as a quite extraordinary and unexampled achievement. (Freud, 1930a, p. 90)

This is what anthropologists call material culture. Moreover, all human activities aim at two intersecting goals: usefulness and plea-sure. But culture must also protect itself from individuals and their destructive, antisocial instincts, just as it must compensate them for the instinctual sacrifices it necessarily imposes upon them, given the fact that it rests on the instinctual renunciation of its participants. This is the purpose of a culture's "mental assets", Freud argued. It is then a matter of finding ways of accommodating two sorts of structurally antagonistic claims, individual and collective,

A good part of the struggles of mankind centre round the single task of finding an expedient accommodation—one, that is, that will bring happiness—between this claim of the individual and the cultural claims of the group; and one of the problems that touches the fate of humanity is whether such an accommodation can be reached by means of some particular form of civilization or whether this conflict is irreconcilable. (Freud, 1930a, p. 96)

"What features of human life must be called cultural"? Or an "overall picture" of culture

This is a question that Freud raised in *Civilization and Its Discontents*. However, he had already provided some invaluable answers in *The Future of an Illusion*. So, with him, we shall look at the material facets, then the ideal, or "cultural psychological" facets, and finally the social facets of this matter. Freud wrote,

We recognize, then, that countries have attained a high level of civi-lization if we find that in them everything which can assist in the exploitation of the earth by man and in his protection against the forces of nature—everything in short, which is of use to him . . . . But we demand other things from civilization . . . we welcome it as a sign of civilization as well if we see people directing their care to what has no practical value whatever, to what is useless . . . . (Freud, 1930a, p. 92)

Indeed, among the traits characteristic of culture, Freud primarily discussed and differentiated the vitally important domain of useful activities aimed at controlling the forces of nature, at obtaining the necessities of life, therefore, at preserving and protecting the human community, the quality of which would determine its "level of culture", from the domain of activities said to be useless, but not without importance, among which figures what pertains to beauty, but also to cleanliness and order. They represent other "requirements" or "demands" that people make of their culture. So it is that, contrary to nature, the requirement of cleanliness is expected both of the culture and of our own bodies.

Then associated with that are the respect, the care, and the leading role bestowed upon ideas, higher intellectual activities, cultural attainments, and creations or "mental assets", the prevalence of which defines a society's degree of culture, among which Freud mentions above all religious systems or "illusions", then philosophical speculation, scientific accomplishments, and artistic creations, and finally, mankind's "ideal-formations", or "store of ideals", of which he wrote:

> The ego ideal opens up an important avenue for the understanding of group psychology. In addition to its individual side, this ideal has a social side; it is also the common ideal of a family, a class, or a nation. It binds not only a person's narcissistic libido, but also a considerable amount of his homosexual libido, which is in this way turned back into the ego. (Freud, 1914c, p. 101)

In *The Future of an Illusion* (Freud, 1927c), Freud invites us to suppose, on the one hand, that these ideals first of all determine the cultural achievements of a society, and on the other hand, that these ideals can just as well be formed from the earlier achievements that are then retained by them so as to be perpetuated. The satisfaction provided by these ideals, or by the ideal, to those participating in the culture is therefore narcissistic in nature and based on pride in an already successful achievement. Freud states,

> To make this satisfaction complete calls for a comparison with other cultures which have aimed at different achievements and have developed different ideals. On the strength of these differences every culture claims the right to look down on the rest. In this way cultural ideals become a source of discord and enmity between different cultural units, as can be seen most clearly in the case of nations. (Freud, 1927c, p. 13)

Consequently, this same narcissistic satisfaction represents one of the means able to neutralise hostility towards one's own culture and to unify a social community in its virtually conflictual diversity by an authorised displacement towards the outside by way of compensation for the wrongs and sacrifices endured.

Freud also discussed the creation of the human superego as a "special mental agency" and "cultural asset in the psychological field". The human mind has undergone a development that is seen in the progressive internalisation of external constraints that has found expression in the creation of a psychic agency, the human superego, which adopts it among its dictates. We can observe this process of transformation in every child, who only becomes moral and social by that means. This creation-establishment of the superego is a "most precious cultural asset in the psychological field". The people in which it has taken place, opponents of civilisation they once were, become *vehicles of culture*, from whence also the idea of "participants in the culture". The greater their number in a culture, the more secure it is, and it will be able to do without the means of external constraint. However, Freud emphasised, the degree of this internalisation varies greatly from one instinctual prohibition to another (Freud, 1927c, pp. 11, 13).

Apart from these *material* and *ideal or mental* facets of culture, Freud looked at the question of modes of regulating social relationships, all the while inquiring into the properly cultural nature of this domain. Would the first attempt to regulate social relationships have been cultural in nature? He considered that it pertained to morals or ethics, one of humanity's first socio-cultural institutions contemporaneous with religion, law, and social organisation, all correlative to totemic culture, the first phase of the phylogenesis of culture. So, this regulation of social relationships is one of the manifestations of a collective agency named by Freud, the cultural superego, which he defined as follows,

> It can be asserted that the community, too, evolves a super-ego under whose influence cultural development proceeds . . .. The super-ego of an epoch of civilization has an origin similar to that of an individual. It is based on the impression left behind by the personalities of great leaders—men of overwhelming force of mind or men in whom one of the human impulsions has found its strongest and purest, and therefore often its most one-sided, expression. (Freud, 1930a, p. 141)

Then he continues explaining,

> The cultural super-ego has developed its ideals and set up its demands. Among the latter, those which deal with the relations of human beings to one another are comprised under the heading of ethics .... Ethics is thus to be regarded as a therapeutic attempt—as an endeavour to achieve, by means of a command of the super-ego, something which has so far not been achieved by means of any other cultural activities. (Freud, 1930a, p. 142)

Cultural development and process

Cultural process, vital process

In *Civilization and Its Discontents*, Freud reflects upon the issues surrounding the development of culture, then culture itself, as a "special process which mankind undergoes" "in the service of Eros, whose purpose is to combine single human individuals, and after that families, then races, peoples and nations, into one great unity, the unity of mankind" by libidinal ties. This is the work of Eros (Freud, 1930a, p. 122). This process is characterised by "the changes which it brings about in the familiar instinctual dispositions of human beings, to satisfy which is, after all, the economic task of our lives" (Freud, 1930a, p. 96). It is comparable to the individual's libidinal development or normal maturation. From this perspective, the sublimation "of instinct is an especially conspicuous feature of cultural development; it is what makes it possible for higher psychical activities, scientific, artistic or ideological, to play such an important part in civilized life" (Freud, 1930a, p. 97).

But standing in opposition to the Eros' programme is the human instinct of destruction. That is why Freud considered that the cultural development, then culture itself, is a process resulting from struggle between Eros and the instinct of destruction, corresponding to the essential content of life, hence the following idea of an analogy between cultural process and organic process, a vital process. Thus, both humanity's cultural process and individual development are vital processes. In this way, one comes to the interrelationships and analogies between the three essential domains to which humanity, the human species, belongs: the biological, the psychical, and the socio-cultural. Freud ultimately asserted that, the process of civilization is a modification which the vital process experiences under the influence of a task that is set it by Eros and instigated by Ananke—by the exigencies of reality; and that this task is one of uniting separate individuals into a community bound together by libidinal ties. When, however, we look at the relation between the process of human civilization and the developmental or educative process of individual human beings, we shall conclude without much hesitation that the two are very similar in nature, if not the very same process applied *to* different kinds of object. (Freud, 1930a, pp. 139–140, my emphasis)

Hence Eros and Ananke as parents of human culture.

Finally, culture, the work of Eros, and in its service, but also the "necessary course of development from the family to humanity as a whole" is connected with the augmentation of the sense of guilt "as a result of the inborn conflict arising from ambivalence, and the eternal struggle between love and death" (Freud, 1930a, p. 133). This is the only way it can achieve its aims. In doing so, if this sense of guilt proves to be the most efficient means of neutralising the instinct of aggressiveness, it also represents the most important problem in cultural development inasmuch as it is the price to be paid for this progress, which results in an inevitable loss of happiness.

Totemic culture, first phase of human culture and the beginning of it

Here is a bit of "theoretical speculation" that Freud offered us.

It was organic repression that paved the way to culture and, in particular, caused anal erotism to succumb. The cultural process was ushered in when human beings began to walk upright, which led to a whole set of correlative phenomena, such as: the decreased importance of olfactory stimuli, through which anal erotism succumbed to the cultural trend toward cleanliness and conditioned it; the prevalence of visual stimuli; visibility of the genital organs hidden up until then and from then on needing protection; the arousal of feelings of shame; isolation during the menstrual period; continuity of sexual excitation, up to the founding of the primitive family and through that to the threshold of human culture. This primitive family or primal horde was dominated by the father's omnipotence. His collective killing by a band of sons–brothers produced a creative sense of guilt and marked the advent of *totemic culture*, the first stage of human culture. How did Freud describe it?

The brothers' organisation, based as it was on homosexual feelings and activities very probably put in place at the time of their ousting, thus created out of the "sons' creative sense of guilt" the two basic taboos of totemism, which could not but tally with the two repressed wishes of the Oedipus complex. Freud considered that human morality began with these two primordial taboos, which are not psychologically equivalent. Since the father's elimination was actually irreparable, the prohibition against killing the totem animal was therefore entirely based on "emotional reasons". It was "religious". While prohibition against incest, by which the brothers renounced the women they desired, enabled them to preserve their burgeoning organisation, just as the prohibition of fratricide did, ruling out, de facto, a recurrence of the father's fate. It was, therefore, social in nature.

According to the anthropologist Maurice Godelier (Godelier, 2004), this totemic culture consequently led to the emergence within this new form of the social organisation of kinship ties as both ties of descent (the descendants of the same totem, of the same blood) and ties of alliance (the groups with which men exchanged the women they had renounced). He observed that this was the very theory formulated by Levi-Strauss in 1949 in *The Elementary Structures of Kinship*! (Levi-Strauss, 1949, p. 14–15).

Thus, this "totemic system" constituted not only a contract with the father, but also a contract among brothers or a social contract. The first form of religion, totemic religion, then the later religions, are based on this contract with the father, which I have expanded upon in the section devoted to the institution of religion. This tenuous, dogmatic Freudian theory has been regularly and vigorously contested by anthropologists and specialists of religions.

Where do things stand with the *social contract* among the brothers?

Their ambivalence being of the enduring kind, the brothers also periodically felt the need to recall the satisfaction felt over their triumph over the father through the ritual ceremony of the totem meal, expressing then an attitude of filial rebelliousness during which the primal criminal collective deed was *symbolised* by the sacrifice of that totem animal, the devouring of which enabled the brothers to acquire the qualities of the dead father, which was one of the goals of the criminal deed.

But this ritual totem meal also reinforced the blood ties of the brothers' community, who identified with one another all the more because they were consuming the same paternal substance, hence the brother's clan's identity of substance. Indeed, its binding force was attributed to drinking and eating together and needed to be repeated to strengthen it and make it permanent. This idea, Freud suggested, was the basis of all the blood alliances conditioning obligations among human beings. Fraternal social feelings were therefore expressed in this sanctification of common blood in reciprocal social obligations, but also in the equal rights enjoyed by the brothers. It is worth noting that this theory was to a large extent inspired by ideas formulated by William Robertson Smith in his *Lectures on the Religion of the Semites* (Smith, 1889), which also won over and influenced Emile Durkheim.

Thus, the communal life of human beings had a twofold foundation:

- Through the compulsion to work created by external necessity. Human beings had discovered that collective work, labour in society according to Durkheim, which would imply and require division of tasks, was an essential means of improving their existence and also conditioned interest in a communal life.
- And through the power of love, the change of egoism into altruism, the woman as man's sexual object, the child as a part of the woman "which had been separated off from her" (Freud, 1930a, p. 101).

Facets of subsequent evolution

However, love, as well as women and the family, would come into conflict with culture. Indeed, the family would clash with the growing unification and complexity of culture all the more so as the solidarity of its members was tight and it was inclined to isolate itself socially. Thus, as Freud explained,

> Detaching himself from his family becomes a task that faces every young person, and society often helps him in the solution of it by means of puberty and initiation rites. We get the impression that these are difficulties which are inherent in all psychical—and, indeed, at bottom, in all organic development. (Freud, 1930a, p. 101)

In this development of humanity, Freud further considered that sensuality was gradually overwhelmed by intellectuality, just as patriarchy would replace matriarchy. He, in fact, observed that the development of language procured for humanity a pride expressing itself in a belief in the "omnipotence of thoughts" (Freud, 1930a, p. 250), particularly in children, neurotic adults, and among primitive peoples, something clearly conducive to openness to intellectuality and intellectual activities to the detriment of sensuality, and "one of the most important stages on the path to humanization" (Freud, 1939a, p. 113). Finally, Freud found that parallel to the progressive control of the world by human beings, their world view was evolving, moving progressively away from the original belief in omnipotence and ascending from the animist phase, by way of the religious phase, to the scientific phase, thus adopting the schema proposed by the British evolutionist anthropologists Edward Burnett Tylor (creator of the concept of animism) and James G. Frazer.

Trans-generational psychical dimension of culture and "organised inherited endowment"

Freud considered that culture was built upon repressions effectuated by earlier generations and that each new generation was obliged to preserve that culture by engaging in those same forms of repression, something that highlights the trans-generational dimension of culture and its processes of transmission, repressions among them, inviting us to conceive of a sort of *transmission activity that is as intrapsychical— individual—as it is collective*, that Rene Kaës (Kaës, 1993) identified well and sought to define. I shall return to this later. But Freud was inquiring into their origin. Are they determined by upbringing and example? Do they have another source in children? He hypothesised that when they establish themselves independently of both,

> a primaeval and prehistoric demand has at last become part of the *organized and inherited endowment of mankind*. A child who produces instinctual repressions spontaneously is thus merely repeating a part of the history of civilization. What is to-day an act of internal restraint was once an external one, imposed, perhaps, by necessities of the moment. (Freud, 1913j, pp. 188–189, my emphasis)

Culture and neurosis

If the foundations of culture condition and favour the upsurge of a neurosis in its members, in particular through coercing instinctual restrictions, and if the analogy between cultural and individual development especially based upon certain similar processes is a valid one, Freud felt justified in inferring the possible existence of *neurotic* cultures and cultural eras under the influence of "the trends of the culture" itself.

Synthetic view of Freudian culture

Undertaking to provide an initial synthesis of the Freudian view-conception of culture, I would say this:

- It has been "human intellectual activity" that has built culture and produced its diverse creations. It has been a matter of collective work on the part of the human community.
- Freud stressed its libidinal, instinctual foundations, the instinctual renunciation required, but also the remodelling and capacity for displacement and sublimation of sexual instincts. In addition he pointed out that this same libidinal activity is also at work in the "causation" of neuroses.
- The essential thing in culture is to control nature in order to procure for oneself the necessities of life with acts and technology guided by scientific knowledge.
- After having defined culture as a system to protect oneself against the dangers of nature, but also for controlling it, with a view towards obtaining the necessities of life, referring to useful material activities of life as a whole, therefore to the "material culture" of the anthropologists, Freud discussed cultural activities said to be "useless", but nevertheless necessary, those pertaining to beauty, order, and cleanliness. Then, he differentiated between "ideal", "mental", and social facets.
- Among those ideal aspects falling into the category of "mental assets", Freud discussed religious ideas, philosophical speculations, scientific discoveries, artistic creations, and then the store of ideal formations or cultural ideals providing compensation for instinctual sacrifices and the agency of the superego, "cultural asset in the psychological field". It is the cultural superego that produces these ideals and sets up its demands.
- As for the social aspects, they concern the modes of regulating social relationships through morals or ethics, one of the manifestations of the cultural superego.

- However, he acknowledged that, all in all, his description was completely classic and unoriginal.

He proposed a dynamic view of culture as a "process", the work of Eros that *drives* people *to establish libidinal ties* with one another so as to form great social units, while remaining subject to Ananke, real necessity, therefore, external reality. This process develops on the scale of humanity and seems analogous to individual development and organic processes. The cultural process takes its place as one of the phenomena of life. It also pertains to the struggle between Eros and the instinct of destruction.

In addition, he offers us a developmental view of culture and a founding myth. The first stage is totemism, therefore totemic culture.

The trans-generational psychical dimension of culture is also essential, with the hypothesis that it is built upon repressions effected by earlier generations and that each new generation is required to participate in maintaining that culture by engaging in the same forms of repression, something that implies the hypothesis of individual and collective work of transmission.

Freud also introduced the idea of the existence of a "mass psyche" and an "organised inherited endowment", both bearing witness to the modalities of intergenerational transmission, therefore of acquisition of a culture.

Other contributions Freud made involve the relationship between culture and individual and collective neurosis. And, in fact, he envisaged the existence of social neuroses or collective neuroses, or of pathology of cultural communities.

Finally, he looked at the relationships between culture and the difference between the sexes.

Before exploring the different institutions that Freud identified starting from the advent of totemic culture, I propose we tour the field of symbolism.

About symbolism

In his *Introductory Lectures on Psycho-Analysis* (Parts I and II), Freud defined the symbolic relationship as a "constant relation . . . between a dream-element and its translation" and described "the dream-element itself as a 'symbol' of the unconscious dream-thought" (Freud, 1915–1916, p. 150). He considered that,

> there is no necessity to assume that any peculiar symbolizing activity of the mind is operating in the dream-work, but that dreams make use of any symbolizations which are already present in unconscious thinking, because they fit in better with the requirements of dream-construction . . .. (Freud, 1900a, p. 349)

Symbolism is, in fact, a second, independent, factor in dream-distortion, of which censorship readily makes use, because it also leads to the dream's strangeness and incomprehensibility. Moreover, "already present" means available right from the beginning of the every dreamer's life.

The essence of this type of relation is a relation of thought, of comparisons of a particular kind among diverse objects, meaning that one can constantly be put in the place of the other. They are all already present and completed once and for all, which is attested to by their matching in diverse persons, overcoming the diversity of languages.

Many symbols common elsewhere do not appear in dreams, or very rarely do, and those of dreams are absent, or not very numerous, in other domains. Thus, in these other domains, the symbolism is not in any way just sexual symbolism, while in dreams symbols are almost exclusively used to express objects and sexual relations. Indeed, except for the human body as a whole, the human person, parents, children, brothers and sisters, birth, death, nudity, it is the realm of sexual life—genital organs, sexual processes, sexual relations—that is represented by a particularly rich symbolism, so that the vast majority of symbols in dreams are sexual symbols. Consequently, Freud observed a distinct contrast between the wealth of sexual symbols and the dearth of things symbolised by multiple, quasi-equivalent symbols, hence a multivocity of symbols and a sameness of interpretations. And he could not help but assume the existence of a particularly close relationship between genuine symbols and sexuality.

The ultimate meaning of this symbolic relation is genetic in nature. According to Freud, "Things that are symbolically connected to-day were probably united in prehistoric times by conceptual and linguistic identity. The symbolic relation seems to be a relic and a mark of former identity" (Freud, 1900a, p. 352). It is therefore a matter of an ancient mode of expression that has disappeared, but of which some elements have been retained in diverse domains in sometimes slightly modified forms, something that suggests, to borrow Daniel Paul Schreber's expression, a "basic language" (Freud, 1911c, pp. 20–27), all the symbolic relations of which would be relics.

But then, Freud asked, where does our knowledge of the meaning of the symbols and symbolic relations of dreams—of which dreamers give us no, or so little, information—come from?

Not specific to dreams and shared, as it happens, with psycho-neurotics, this symbolism is, in fact, part of the "unconscious representational activity" of peoples and thus we find it again in folklore, diverse customs and practices, folk languages, but also in myths, stories, and legends. Once again connecting up with Durkheim's thought, Freud ultimately discussed the unconscious symbolic language of societies. Its domain, of course, consequently includes that of individuals and their culture, external and internalised in each of its participants. So, through this field of symbolism, a link is established between these two orders of reality, individual and collective, something justifying for Freud psychoanalysis' central position between psychopathology and the cultural sciences.

About some institutions

After having attempted to define and characterise social and cultural institutions from the Freudian perspective, I shall now present the main ones, those he mentioned right from the start of *totemic culture*, the first phase of the development of human culture, then in the course of his writings: religion, morality or ethics, and law. As for art, its place fluctuated, but Freud presented it elsewhere as an institution. I shall therefore approach it as such. He considered that they had been established together and were interdependent, something that implies a beginning of organisation into a system. But unlike sociologists such as Durkheim and Mauss, Freud would not go to the point of conceptualising the notion of system.

Religion

Genesis and evolution of Freud's thoughts about religion based on *Totem and Taboo* and *Moses and Monotheism*.

Totemic religion or the totemic system

In *Totem and Taboo*, Freud tells of the psychological conditions and very beginnings of the religion-institution by stressing, in particular, the following points. First of all, the first form of religion, totemic religion, then the later religions, are based on the *contract with the father*. The ambivalence inherent in the father-complex is characterised as much by hostility having determined the brothers' collective criminal deed, as by a flow of affection at the origin of the sons' feelings of guilt and their displays of repentance. Religion would then be an attempt at appeasing those feelings and at reconciliation with the offended father through obedience after the fact. In addition, the father should provide "everything that the childish imagination may expect from a father—protection, care and indulgence—while on their side they undertook to respect his life" (Freud, 1912–1913, p. 144). Totemism also involved an attempt at self-justification: "If our father had treated us in the way the totem does, we should never have felt tempted to kill him" (Freud, 1912–1913, p. 145).

Starting with totemism, what are the features determining the nature of religion?

Once hatred had been satisfied by the criminal deed, the other feeling, love, found expression in collective remorse for that deed, set up the superego through identification with the father, conferred the father's power upon it, as if in punishment for that criminal deed committed against him, and established the founding prohibition forbidding a repetition of the heinous crime.

Freud consequently maintained that all religions are reactions to that great event owing to which culture began, are attempts to solve the same problem, varying in each case as a function of the cultural situation in which they were made and as a function of the course they adopted. They all have the same goal. The ambivalence inherent in the father-complex continued in religions in general. Apart from the displays of repentance, there was in addition the memory of triumph over the father, the satisfaction over which led to the institution of the commemorative celebration represented by the totemic meal, ritually repeating the murder of the father by sacrificing the totem-animal and eating it, which enabled the sons–brothers to acquire the qualities possessed by the father, which must not completely disappear. In so doing, the social fraternal feelings were strengthened all the more by the eating of the common paternal substance, which contributed to the sanctification of the clan's common blood. However, a part of the filial rebelliousness also reappears in the most extraordinary disguises and transformations in later religious phenomena.

Starting with totemism, the evolution that followed pertains to the manifestation of a "slow return of what had been repressed" as affected by all the changes occurring in living conditions, changes with which, incidentally, human cultural history is replete. This evolution was oriented towards the humanisation of the venerated being. The totem-animal gave way to the god in transitions marked by polytheistic stages. Great maternal deities appeared, probably at the time of the restriction of the matriarchy, as a compensation for mothers being relegated to the side-lines, then persisted during the appearance of male deities, first of all as sons alongside great mothers, and later distinctly adopted the traits of paternal figures. In between, a major social upheaval took place. The matriarchy was replaced by a re-established patriarchal system. These male gods reflecting the conditions of the patriarchal era were numerous and deferred at times to a sovereign god placed above them. But the next step led to the return of a single god–father, to unrestricted dominance. This was the advent of Jewish, then Christian, and finally Moslem, monotheism, though Freud never mentioned the latter.

This Freudian approach, which was audacious and speculative to say the least, became a sort of dogma for him. It would of course be hotly contested and rejected by anthropologists, sociologists, and religious scholars, in particular owing to its failure to differentiate between the historical forms of religions, but also owing to his failure to take into consideration cultural, economic, political, and social contexts. Freud considered religions to be psychical facts, and not socio-cultural, historically determined facts, interdependent with other social facts. He was likewise unable to envisage their symbolical nature and their incorporation into systems said to be symbolical, like languages, for example.

Sacredness, the sacred and religious phenomena

Everything that is religious is sacred. It is quite simply the essence of holiness.

Freud maintained that the sacred was originally nothing other than the perpetuation of the will of the primal father. This also shed light on the ambivalence, incomprehensible up to that point, of the words expressing the concept of sacredness, such as "sacer". In fact, when Moses "made his people holy" by introducing the practice of circumcision, we must understand this as a *symbolical substitute for the castration* that the primal father had decreed for his sons in the past in the fullness of his absolute power, and those adopting this *symbol* in doing so showed themselves ready to obey the father's will in spite of this painful sacrifice.

The analogy between neurotic symptoms and religious phenomena or the transition from individual psychology to group psychology

"Obsessive actions and religious practices"

As Freud wrote,

> I am certainly not the first person to have been struck by the resemblance between what are called obsessive actions in sufferers from nervous affections and the observances by means of which believers give expression to their piety. The term "ceremonial", which has been applied to some of these obsessive actions, is evidence of this. The resemblance, however, seems to me to be more than a superficial one, so that an insight into the origin of neurotic ceremonial may embolden us to draw inferences about the psychological processes of religious life. (Freud, 1907b, p. 117)

In consideration of the points of agreement, analogies, and differences identified—among them, scrupulousness in performing ritual acts, their historical and symbolical meaning, as well as their being founded on a common sense of guilt and their role in providing protection against an instinctual danger—Freud was tempted to qualify the obsessional neurosis of individual religiosity and religion as universal obsessional neurosis. Their fundamental area of agreement would consist in a kind of instinctual renunciation and their essential difference in the nature of the repressed instinctual, phenomena of sexual origin in the case of neurosis and of egoistical origin, "detrimental to society", in the case of religion.

Thus,

> A progressive renunciation of constitutional instincts, whose activation might afford the ego primary pleasure, appears to be one of the

foundations of the development of human civilization. Some part of this instinctual repression is effected by its religions, in that they require the individual to sacrifice his instinctual pleasure to the Deity. (Freud, 1907b, p. 127)

Moses and Monotheism

According to Freud, the formula established for the development of a neurosis (early trauma, defence, latency, outbreak of neurotic illness, partial return of the repressed), is not only applicable to religious phenomena, in particular to the history of Jewish monotheism, but also to the life of the human species, in the course of which things have occurred (operative and forgotten traumas) that are similar to those in the lives of individuals. Indeed, "here too events occurred of a sexually-aggressive nature, which left behind them permanent consequences, but were for the most part fended off and forgotten, and which after a long latency came into effect and created phenomena similar to symptoms in their structure and purpose". This was the case with religious phenomena in particular. He further maintained that there was almost complete agreement between the individual and the group through the latter's retaining of impressions of the past in unconscious memory traces (Freud, 1939a, pp. 80, 94).

New analogy: delusional formation and religion

Freud presents a different understanding of religions in *Civilization and Its Discontents*. There, they involve a "delusional remoulding of reality" or "mass-delusion" (Freud, 1930a, p. 81), and a collective technique for fending off suffering. However, by imposing "equally on everyone its own path", it "restricts this play of choice and adaptation" (Freud, 1930a, p. 84). And its

> technique consists in depressing the value of life and distorting the picture of the real world in a delusional manner—which presupposes the intimidation of the intelligence. At this price, by forcibly fixing them in a state of psychical infantilism and by drawing them into a mass-delusion, religion succeeds in sparing many people an individual neurosis. (Freud, 1930a, pp. 84–85)

Freud identified two sorts of components in the doctrines and rites of the religious tradition: on the one hand, fixations on earlier family history and the legacy of the latter; on the other hand, restoration of the past, the distorted reappearances of what was forgotten, "repressed", after a long period of latency. He also distinguished between two types of tradition: that exclusively based on communication, and that built on those reappearances of forgotten significant events exercising a powerful effect on the masses. He, in fact, observed that "each portion which returns from oblivion asserts itself with peculiar force, exercises an incomparably powerful influence on people in the mass" (Freud, 1939a, p. 85) freed of the constraints of logical thought and aspiring irresistibly to the truth, something understandable, not on the neurotic pattern, but rather in terms of the delusions of psychotics. *Religious doctrines also have a portion of forgotten historical truth, bearing the character of psychotic symptoms of groups.* Thus light is shed, according to Freud, on the history of the development of religion as an institution and tradition, from its first form, totemism, to the monotheisms, going by way of polytheistic stages.

The store of religious representations or one of the "mental assets" of culture

The Future of an Illusion

According to Freud, religious representations are "born from man's need to make his helplessness tolerable", *meaning that state of anxiety and weakness of human beings inherent in the "over-mighty" world of the forces of nature.* A person has "an infantile prototype", that "of memories of the helplessness of his own childhood and the childhood of the human race". These ideas therefore proceed from the same need as culture's other conquests, that of protecting human beings in two directions, against the dangers of the superior power of nature and fate and against distressing injuries inflicted by human society itself. And culture presents and transmits to every individual this "store of religious representations" ready-made. They are already there to be found. (Freud, 1927c, pp. 16–21)

It is a matter of dogmas or doctrines, objects of belief that in their psychological nature, that is to say, in their motivation, are illusions, above all "fulfilments of the oldest, the strongest and most urgent wishes of mankind", correlative to human helplessness and to the persistent longing for the protection provided by the father, embodied in a deity. One cannot make any judgment about the reality-value of most of them, which cannot be proved or refuted, according to Freud. (Freud, 1927c, pp. 30–33)

Why were these religious doctrines created?

Though Freud admitted that, if religion had "performed great services to human civilization", such as that of contributing partially toward the "taming of asocial instincts", he nevertheless observed that after several millennia of dominating human society, it had not really satisfied people's expectations, a large number of whom remain unhappy, wishing to bring about changes in it, even expressing diverse forms of hostility toward it (Freud, 1927c, p. 37).

With a view toward making this social phenomenon intelligible to us through his theories, Freud once again appealed to an analogy between the cultural development of humanity and that of every human child, who necessarily goes through a phase of neurosis. Thus, in the course of its history, humanity has also gone through states "analogous" to neuroses, and for the same reasons, such as the collective instinctual renunciations indispensable to all social life, the "residues" that occurred in prehistoric times would long remain embedded in the culture. Like the child's obsessional neurosis arising out of the paternal Oedipus complex, religion would be a "universal obsessional neurosis of humanity" protecting believers from the danger of forming a personal neurosis. Its teachings would then correspond to *neurotic relics* of one of the phases of the history of the cultural development of humanity. And Freud hoped that his times would witness the triumph of rational, scientific thinking, which would especially help reconcile people with their culture and its dictates finally established on a rational basis.

Consequently, *as a universal obsessional neurosis, religion therefore brings with it obsessional restrictions of a neurotic kind, but it also constitutes a system of illusions, therefore, of wish-fulfilments inherent in a disavowal of reality, which represents its delusional, therefore psychotic, aspect that Freud found in an isolated form* in "*amentia,* in a state of blissful hallucinatory confusion" (Freud, 1927c, pp. 43–44, my emphasis).

Civilization and Its Discontents

Religion is presented to us as participating in and furthering the cultural process, which is principally motivated by the "aim of creating a unity out of individual human beings", the pursuit of happiness becoming consequently secondary. Moreover, the hypothetical evolving of a superego by any society—or cultural superego—is comparable to the individual superego under whose influence cultural development proceeds and, "based on the impression left behind by the personalities of great leaders—men of overwhelming force of mind", is particularly fruitful with regard to the role of any religion. This superego develops its ideals and sets up its demands, among them those concerning the relationships of human beings to one another or social relationships falling under the heading of ethics. In this manner, religious phenomena become intelligible through an understanding of the influence of the cultural superego (Freud, 1930a, pp. 140–142).

The religious Weltanschauung, Lecture XXXV

The "grandiose nature of religion" lies in the fulfilment of three functions corresponding to the satisfaction of fundamental human needs: satisfying the thirst for knowledge; soothing the fear human beings feel before the dangers and vicissitudes of life and providing comfort in times of unhappiness; and finally issuing precepts, prohibitions, and restrictions by way of rules for conducting one's life. *It is an attempt to master the sensory world by means of the still alive wishful world of childhood* that we have developed within ourselves as a result of "psychological and biological necessities" (Freud, 1933a, Lecture XXXV, pp. 161, 168).

However, in the name of self-preservation, religion issues a prohibition against thought, which has a tendency to widen and thus cause severe inhibitions in the ways individuals conduct their lives. Freud deplored this and that is why he demanded that the ultimate aim of reason or the scientific spirit be to establish in the course of time "a dictatorship in the mental life of man", which could then assign a proper place to human feelings. He also expected that this would have a "unifying influence on men . . . whom it is . . . scarcely possible to rule" (Freud, 1933a, Lecture XXXV, p. 171).

The "Christian group" as an example of a community and a religious institution

Within the Christian Church as an "artificial" group with a leader, the illusion reigns that Christ loves all individuals with an equal love.

This type of group is based, on the one hand, on aim-inhibited libidinal ties and identifications among the believing members made possible by the same relationship to the leader (Christ, God, teachings) and, on the other hand, on the replacement of each one's ego ideal by that object-leader, while the social feeling reigning within this group rests on changing an initial feeling of hostile rivalry into identification on the basis of a common ego ideal, as well as on the sharing of common beliefs and the performing of rites.

It also presupposes some conditions and repercussions for each of them, setting limits on their narcissism, therefore, on their peculiarities, in favour of their similarities and of their love for the object, something that can but inhibit the hostility arising out of narcissistic self-affirmation intolerant of the slightest difference, which will find satisfaction outside the group. Thus, as Freud emphasised, "every religion is in this same way a religion of love for all those whom it embraces; while cruelty and intolerance towards those who do not belong to it are natural to every religion" (Freud, 1921c, p. 98).

Depicted in this manner, characterised by the image of an exceedingly strong individual (Christ, God) within a group of equal individuals, this "Christian group" was suggestive to Freud of a regressive representation of the primal horde, but also of its revival through a "religious group".

Religiosity and oceanic feeling

According to Romain Rolland, religiosity is a particular feeling that he would be ready to call the sensation of "eternity", a feeling of something limitless, boundless, "oceanic" as it were, a purely subjective fact, source of religious energy that is tapped, steered into specific channels and certainly even totally absorbed by the diverse Churches and religious systems. It is a feeling of belonging to the totality of the external world. Freud considered that one may "rightly call oneself religious on the ground of this oceanic feeling alone, even if one rejects every belief and every illusion" (Freud, 1930a, p. 64).

Freud traced this "oceanic feeling" back to an early phase, that of primal narcissism, of the feeling of the ego in close connection with the surrounding world, first of all the mother, and then back to the helplessness of childhood. He wrote, "The 'oneness with the universe' which constitutes its ideational content sounds like a first attempt at a religious consolation as though it were another way of disclaiming the danger which the ego recognizes as threatening it from the external world" (Freud, 1930a, p. 72).

Religion and education

Freud invited us to reflect on the role of religion in education, but more profoundly on its contribution to structuring the psyche of every child, as well as on its offering sublimational solutions and a path to socialisation.

The situation of the 'Wolfman'

Religion is included in the education of the individual as much through the taming of sexual impulses, which through sublimation are diverted to spiritual ones offering another form of satisfaction, as through access to the social relationships that it offers to believers (Freud, 1918b, pp. 114–115), thus enabling every child to achieve necessary detachment from its family.

The Future of an Illusion

Freud considered that these religious doctrines are imposed on "children, who are driven by instinct and weak in intellect" (Freud, 1927c, p. 51) at a most premature time in their intellectual development, that is to say when they are neither interested in them nor *able to grasp the diverse messages*. As he explained, "*Is it not true that the two main points in the programme* for the education of children to-day are the retardation of sexual development and premature religious influence? Thus by the time the child's intellect awakens, the doctrines of religion have already become unassailable" (Freud, 1927c, pp. 47–48, my emphasis).

By way of conclusion

Freud, fervent rationalist that he was, drew conclusions about the progress that needed to be made. Religion maintains all human beings in a perpetual childlike state. Yet, they "must in the end go out into 'hostile life' ", which amounts to an "education to reality". People are not without help. They have their own resources, scientific progress.

They must free themselves from their expectations regarding the other world, concentrate all the energies thus liberated on life on this planet, endure with resignation the great necessities of fate. Thenceforth, life could be bearable for everyone (Freud, 1927c, pp. 49–50).

Morals, morality, ethics

Translation

> *Moral* = morals
> *Moralität* and *Sittlichkeit* = morality
> *Ethik* = ethics

According to Jean Laplanche, a careful reading of Freud's writings does not reveal any difference between the two groups of terms. Thus, *moralisches Gewissen=sittliches Gewissen=*"conscience". Only the term *Sitten* retains a more sociological meaning in his thought and designates "mores", non-internalised standards (Laplanche, 1989, pp. 117–118).

Let us now look at the other institution regularly mentioned by Freud, morals or ethics, a term introduced in around the 1920s along with a socio-cultural tool communicated by families with a view to its acquisition and intrapsychical-individual internalisation: education.

Some lexical aspects

> "Religious morality"; "sexual morality"; "moral inhibitions"; "moral order", "fundamental moral limitations"; moral prescriptions; moral requirements of a stage of culture; conscience, moral standards; notion of "group morality"; "moralization of the individual by the group"; "moral relationships among collective-individuals".
>
> "The ego's ethical demands"; "ethical restrictions"; ethical behaviour; ethical precepts; the ethical development of children; ethical commands; requirements said to be ethical by human culture; ethical level.

First occurrences

One of the first occurrences of the noun *morality* or the adjective *moral* is found in 1893 in *Studies on Hysteria,*

Thus the mechanism which produces hysteria represents on the one hand *an act of moral cowardice* and on the other a defensive measure which is at the disposal of the ego ... more frequently, of course, we shall conclude that a greater amount of moral courage would have been of advantage to the person concerned. (Freud, 1895d, p. 123, my emphasis)

Allow me also to mention "Draft K, the neuroses of defence from extracts from the Fliess Papers" (January 1, 1896) (Freud, 1892), where Freud separated shame, morality, and disgust, the first two being defined as "repressing forces" exerted on premature sexual experience.

The notion of "sexual morality" appeared for the first time in 1898 in "Sexuality in the aetiology of the neuroses", and we find it again later in 1905 in *Three Essays on the Theory on Sexuality*, but especially in 1908 in " 'Civilized' sexual morality and modern nervous illness". In "Sexuality in the aetiology of the neuroses", he wrote,

Moreover, it is in the interest of all of us that a higher degree of honesty about sexual things should become a duty among men and women than has hitherto been expected of them. This cannot be anything but a gain for *sexual morality*. In matters of sexuality we are at present, every one of us, ill or well, nothing but hypocrites. It will be all to our good if, as a result of such general honesty, a certain amount of toleration in sexual concerns should be attained. (Freud, 1898a, p. 266, my emphasis)

Some elements of the Freudian definition of morals and ethics

Freud at first used the term morality, and it was only in the 1920s that he introduced the notion of ethics. It is curious to observe that he fairly often combined the adjectives "ethical" or "moral" and "aesthetic" with the ego's "tendencies, obstacles or demands" determining the repression of irreconcilable representations. He wrote that "we have from the very beginning attributed the function of instigating repression to the moral and aesthetic trends in the ego" (Freud, 1923b, p. 35).

Morality, ethics, is an *instinctual restriction*, Freud affirmed. He maintained this and repeated it on numerous occasions. Thus, in "Dostoevsky and parricide", he maintained that,

A moral man is one who reacts to temptation as soon as he feels it within his heart, without yielding to it. A man who alternately sins and then in his remorse erects high moral standards lays himself open to the reproach that he has made things too easy for himself. He has not achieved the essence of morality, renunciation, for the moral conduct of life is a practical human interest. (Freud, 1928b, p. 177)

Then, in *Moses and Monotheism*, he wrote of morality that "a part of its precepts are justified rationally by the necessity for delimiting the rights of society as against the individual, the rights of the individual as against society and those of individuals as against one another" (Freud, 1939a, p. 122).

Morality as one of the first, social and cultural human institutions

Origin and phylogenesis

In *Totem and Taboo* (Freud, 1912–1913), Freud discussed the establishment of morality in human beings correlative to the creation of the two fundamental taboos of totemism from the sons' sense of guilt after the killing of the father of the primal horde. These two psychically non-equivalent taboos correspond to two repressed wishes of the Oedipus complex. These first moral *prescriptions* and *limitations* of the fraternal clan or totemic society—reacting to a criminal deed that must not be repeated, the prohibition against killing and incest—or *first form of human morality*, were therefore based "partly on the exigencies of this society, and partly on the penance demanded by the sense of guilt" (Freud, 1912–1913, p. 146). In this way, one of the first human institutions declared to be "sacred" or "imperishable" was established concurrently and in connection with those of religion, law, and art— became inherent in the Oedipus complex—making possible the organisation of a "social moral order". Freud moreover presents there his reconstruction of a history of taboos and of the conscience.

About the history of taboos

Having appealed to the analogy with obsessional neurosis, Freud imagined that these prohibitions concerning objects of desire and temptation were violently imposed and inculcated in a generation of primitive people by the previous generation. He inquired into the ways in which they were preserved and transmitted to later generations, be it through tradition doubly ensured by parental and social authority, but also in keeping with Lamarckian theories, in this instance, through the "hereditary transmission of acquired mental characteristics", these prohibitions being " 'organized' as an inherited psychical endowment" (Freud, 1912–1913, p. 31). He also emphasised the persistence of an ambivalent attitude taken towards these fundamental prohibitions.

About the conscience and its genesis in Freud's thought

After having established a necessary distinction between a taboo conscience and a taboo consciousness of guilt after transgressing taboos, Freud considered that the conscience as we know it originated phylogenetically in the taboo conscience and defined it as follows,

> Conscience is the internal perception of the rejection of a particular wish operating within us. The stress, however, is on the fact that this rejection has no need to appeal to anything else for support, that it is quite "certain of itself". This is even clearer in the case of consciousness of guilt—the perception of the internal condemnation of an act by which we have carried out a particular wish. To put forward any reason for this would seem superfluous: anyone who has a conscience must feel within him the justification for the condemnation, must feel the self-reproach for the act that has been carried out. This same characteristic is to be seen in the savage's attitude towards taboo . . . .

> Thus it seems probable that conscience too arose, on a basis of emotional ambivalence, from quite specific human relations to which this ambivalence was attached; and that it arose under the conditions which we have shown to apply in the case of taboo and of obsessional neurosis . . . . (Freud, 1912–1913, p. 68)

Collective morality, that of "groups", peoples, and states

Every society prescribes "moral standards" or "standards of morality" for its members, in accordance with which they will have to adjust the way they lead their lives and enabling them to be "participants in the culture". In particular, they require of them "much self-restraint, much renunciation of instinctual satisfaction" (Freud, 1915b, p. 276), without compensation for the sacrifice required.

"The civilized states," Freud explained, "regarded these moral standards as the basis of their existence. They took serious steps if anyone ventured to tamper with them, and often declared it improper even to subject them to examination by a critical intelligence" (Freud, 1915b, p. 276).

He introduced the notion of "ethical relations" among the "collective-individuals" represented by peoples or states, then that of "morals of a group" in "Group psychology and the analysis of the ego" (Freud, 1921c, p. 82). He then discussed the possibility of the falling off of these "ethical relations" among peoples, an abandonment of their moral restraint that particularly finds expression in wars with their inevitable repercussions on the morality of individuals reflected in tolerance of uninhibited behaviour. He noted, "When the community no longer raises objections, there is an end, too, to the suppression of evil passions, and men perpetrate deeds of cruelty, fraud, treachery and barbarity" (Freud, 1915b, p. 280).

And added that the,

> fact that the collective-individuals of mankind, the peoples and states, mutually abrogated their moral restraints naturally prompted these individual citizens to withdraw for a while from the constant pressure of civilization and to grant a temporary satisfaction to the instincts which they had been holding in check. This probably involved no breach in their relative morality within their own nations. (Freud, 1915b, p. 285)

It is then that Freud reflected and came to believe that the morality of peoples and states is less developed than that of any individual, corresponding then to one of the "primitive stages of development". He observed that "the educative factor of an external compulsion towards morality, which we found was so effective in individuals, is as yet barely discernible in them ... it would seem that nations still obey their passions far more readily than their interests" (Freud, 1915b, p. 288).

Yet, every society evolves a *cultural superego* which produces its ideals and its demands, the latter involving social relationships are comprised under the heading of ethics. He defined its precise role and purpose in *Civilization and Its Discontents*, writing, "As we already know, the problem before us is how to get rid of the greatest hindrances to civilization—namely, the constitutional inclinational of human beings to be aggressive towards one another" (Freud, 1930a, p. 142).

Individuals and their morals or individual morality

The notions of good and bad

The morality of every person refers to notions of good and bad, to the need to learn to distinguish between them. In *Civilization and Its Discontents*, Freud shed some fairly relevant light on their socio-cultural dimension and significance as transmitted by the family institution. He wrote,

> We may reject the existence of an original, as it were natural, capacity to distinguish good from bad. What is bad is often not at all what is injurious or dangerous to the ego; on the contrary, it may be something which is desirable and enjoyable to the ego. Here, therefore, there is an extraneous influence at work, and it is this that decides what is to be called good or bad .... At the beginning, therefore, what is bad is whatever causes one to be threatened with loss of love. For fear of that loss, one must avoid it. This, too, is the reason why it makes little difference whether one has already done the bad thing or only intends to do it. In either case, the danger sets in if and when the authority discovers it, and in either case the authority would behave in the same way. This state of mind is called a "bad conscience"; but actually it does not deserve this name, for at this stage the sense of guilt is clearly only a fear of loss of love, "social anxiety". In small children it can never be anything else, but in many adults, too, it has only changed to the extent that the place of the father or the two parents is taken by the larger human community .... A great change takes place only when the authority is internalized through the establishment of a super-ego. The phenomena of conscience then reach a higher stage. Actually it is not until now that we should speak of conscience or a sense of guilt. At this point, too, the fear of being found out comes to an end; the distinction, moreover, between doing something bad and wishing to do it disappears entirely, since nothing can be hidden from the super-ego, not even thoughts. (Freud, 1930a, pp. 124–125)

In addition, Freud reminded us in "The economic problem of masochism" that the Oedipus complex is the source of our individual morality, morals, and the conscience having arisen through its "over-coming" and desexualisation. Indeed, the superego, heir to the Oedipus complex, becomes representative of human ethical requirements (Freud, 1924c, pp. 169–170).

Ontogenesis of morality

Freud described the "little primitive" that is the human child as being an "absolutely egotistical" being intensely feeling imperious needs to be satisfied without any consideration for its rivals, the other children, in particular, its brothers and sisters, therefore dominated by the pleasure principle, without any anxiety regarding the dangers of reality, and, what is more, "polymorphously perverse", "amoral".

In his *Introductory Lectures on Psycho-Analysis* (Part III) (1916–1917), Freud reminded readers that what we call "perversion" in adult life corresponds to an inhibition of sexual development or in an "infantilism" and departs from the normal in the following respects: by crossing the barrier of species (the gulf between animals and humans); by transgression of the barrier against disgust, of the barrier against incest, of belonging to the same sex; finally by transferring the genital role to other organs and places in the body. Since all these barriers do not exist from the beginning, children are therefore exempt from them and can actually be called "polymorphously perverse". They will only be erected in the course of a child's development and education.

"Becoming a moral and social being" is a process that, according to Freud, principally takes place during the period of sexual latency during which those "mental powers" are developed that will bar the route to perverse infantile sexual impulses and which, like dykes, will hold back and channel their flow in the course of the child's development until puberty. It is a matter of disgust, feelings of shame, moral and aesthetic ideal standards. It is curious to observe that, in the course of Freud's work, these "mental powers" and the nature of them would be designated differently, as "obstacles", "aesthetic and ethical barriers", "reactive formations or resistances", "mental inhibitions". Just as shame, modesty would remain, others would appear: pity, social constructions of morals and authority, barrier to incest, etc. In "Three essays on the theory of sexuality", Freud stated that "this development is organically determined and fixed by heredity" and he attributed a secondary role to education, even considering that these processes could "occasionally occur without any help from education". He explained his idea writing, "Education will not be trespassing beyond its appropriate domain if it limits itself to following the lines which have already been laid down organically and to impressing them somewhat more clearly and deeply" (Freud, 1905d, 177–178).

However, he would later abandon the much too biological viewpoint of the *Three Essays on the Theory of Sexuality* to make it more nuanced and to grant interdependent, complementary roles to diverse factors: the child's "constitutional disposition"; biology, owing to the prolonged infantile dependency on parents specific to the human species; parental influence, which would essentially assume the expenditure necessary to repression, therefore the education that the "cultural demands in the family" represents; but also the influence of the "cultural milieu".

In his *Autobiographical Study* (additional note 1935), Freud explained that the period of latency, a physiological phenomenon, can only give rise to "a complete interruption of sexual life in cultural organizations which have made the suppression of infantile sexuality a part of their system. This is not the case with the majority of primitive peoples" (Freud, 1925d, p. 37). This shows that Freud adjusted his views in accordance with his readings, in ethnography, in particular. It is, in fact, imaginable that he was influenced by the writings of Bronislaw Malinowski and Géza Róheim.

Freud considered these "mental constructions" to be particularly significant for every individual's subsequent personal culture and normality.

Law and justice

Translation

> *Recht*=law
> *Mutterrecht*=matriarchy
> *Gerechtigkeit*=justice

Chronological exploration of the texts

The first occurrence of the notion of law in Freud's work occurred in his 1905 study of marriage laws (Freud, 1905), written in connection with a decision made by the imperial government to form a commission charged with revising divorce legislation. He responded to diverse questions on the institution of marriage, relations between the sexes, the effects of continence, or sexual abstinence. Then in "Notes upon a case of obsessional neurosis", he would introduce the notion of the transition from matriarchy to patriarchy that, along with placing inference upon a level with the testimony of the senses, constituted, according him, a "great advance . . . made in civilization" (Freud, 1909d, p. 233).

In *Totem and Taboo*, inspired by the theories of Johann Jakob Bachofen on matriarchies (Bachofen, 1861), Freud took up the origins of human law and its beginnings in the form of matriarchy, which would later be replaced by the patriarchal family order. Indeed, Freud considered that the establishment of the prohibition of incest and the social organisation set up by the brothers' alliance based on sublimated homosexual feelings "may perhaps have been the germ of the institution of matriarchy (Freud, 1912–1913, p. 144).

Furthermore, the notion of justice, which is a "group feeling", appears in Freud's writings in 1921 with "Group psychology and the analysis of the ego". He tells readers of its ontogenesis, considering that it emerged in the bedrooms of children out of sibling envy and jealousy with respect to their parents' love and that the maintaining of a dangerous virtually hostile attitude brought about a change, that of identification with other children, thus creating a "feeling of community" by reactive formation, which would later develop at school, then elsewhere, and whose first demand, Freud emphasised, would be that of justice, therefore of equal treatment for all. He wrote,

> What appears later on in society in the shape of *Gemeingeist*, *esprit de corps*, "group spirit", etc., does not belie its derivation from what was originally envy. No one must want to put himself forward, everyone must be the same and have the same. Social justice means that we deny ourselves many things so that others may have to do without them as well, or, what is the same thing, may not be able to ask for them. This demand for equality is the root of social conscience and the sense of duty. (Freud, 1921c, pp. 120–121)

However, in "Some psychical consequences of the anatomical distinction between the sexes", after having mentioned a difference in the level of morality between men and women, Freud also points out a difference between the sexes when it comes to the sense of justice, alleging that women "show less sense of justice than men, that they are less ready to submit to the great exigencies of life" (Freud, 1925j, pp. 257–258).

Later, in *Civilization and Its Discontents*, he would considerably expand upon his views on justice and law, deeming that it was a question of one of the essential preconditions of all social life, or rather of regulating social relationships.

It was then that Freud introduced his conception of law as "community power", as opposed to "individual power", condemned as "brute violence". And this transition, as well as this replacement of individual power by that of the community based on restricting the opportunities for gratification, was considered by him to be "the decisive step of civilization" (Freud, 1930a, p. 95). From a phylogenetic perspective, this echoes back to the mutative transition from the primal horde or primitive family ruled by an all-powerful father with unlimited free will and—following his collective murder committed by the brothers' alliance—to the organisation of totemic society, first stage of human culture resting on mutual restrictions, a "social contract" with the establishment of humanity's first cultural institutions, among them the "first law" corresponding to the first taboo prescriptions, accompanied by equality of rights for all the brothers of the alliance. According to Freud, "the first requisite of civilization, therefore, is that of justice—that is, the assurance that a law once made will not be broken in favour of an individual" (Freud, 1930a, p. 95).

But this first stage of human law would be the expression solely of the will of a small ruling community behaving as a "violent individual" toward the masses. So, the following stage should be the coming of a law concerning all the members of the community who had contributed by their instinctual sacrifices, consequently, protecting each one of them from brute violence. This is why Freud considered that,

> The liberty of the individual is no gift of civilization. It was greatest before there was any civilization, though then, it is true, it had for the most part no value, since the individual was scarcely in a position to defend it. The development of civilization imposes restrictions on it, and justice demands that no one shall escape those restrictions. (Freud, 1930a, pp. 95–96)

However, Freud remained conscious of the inevitable injustice involved in the fact that nature had very unequally endowed every individual with a body and a mind. In like manner, he advocated "ruling the masses" by a small elite group of "leaders" educated by a "dictatorship of reason" for this purpose.

In 1932, in "Why war?", he reminded readers of the path leading from violence—brute or supported by the intellect—towards law and opposing them, that of the individual's violence against the might of a community, which must remain stable in its organisation, institutions, and laws to be respected.

In so doing, the

> recognition of a community of interests such as these lead to the growth of emotional ties between the members of a united group of people—communal feelings which are the true source of its strength. Here, I believe, we already have all the essentials: violence overcome by the transference of power to a larger unity, which is held together by emotional ties between its members. What remains to be said is no more than an expansion and a repetition of this. (Freud, 1933b, p. 205)

In this manner, the cohesion of a community rests as much on the compelling force of violence as on identifications among its members.

However, Freud sounded the alarm, once again, regarding the dangers of establishing within the community an unequal law that is in the service of the ruling members and an expression of the unequal degrees of power in it, something attesting to sources of unrest, but also to progress.

Freud ultimately found that society could not avoid solving conflicts of interest through violence, whatever its forms, among them war or wars. Resorting to violence remains present. And wars could, moreover, lead to the creation of large units within which a strong central power capable of preventing new wars could be established. Wars have, in fact, not disappeared and wars on a grand scale have replaced numerous minor wars. This is why wars

> will only be prevented with certainty if mankind unites in setting up a central authority to which the right of giving judgement upon all conflicts of interest shall be handed over. There are clearly two separate requirements involved in this: the creation of a supreme agency and its endowment with the necessary power. (Freud, 1933b, p. 207)

These ideas connect up with those formulated by the sociologist Norbert Elias, notably in his *State Formation and Civilization* (Elias, 1939, vol. 2).

In his 1933 text entitled "Femininity", Freud continued to hold that women must be regarded as having little sense of justice and that this is connected with the preponderance of envy in their mental life. For, as he wrote, "the demand for justice is a modification of envy and lays down the precondition subject to which one can put envy aside" (Freud, 1933a, Lecture XXXIII, p. 134).

Finally, in *Moses and Monotheism*, he took up the ideas he had formulated and developed in *Totem and Taboo*, according to which humanity's social evolution is characterised by the transition from matriarchy to patriarchy, but he does not substantiate this. There, he understood it as a slow "return of the repressed" taking place,

> under the influence of all the changes in conditions of life which fill the history of modifications of human civilization . . .. The father once more became the head of the family, but was not by any means so absolute as the father of the primal horde had been. (Freud, 1939a, p. 133)

And for Freud this victory of the law of the father represented an "advance in intellectuality" that

> consists in deciding against direct sense-perception in favour of what is known as the higher intellectual processes—that is memories, reflections and inferences. It consists, for instance, in deciding that paternity is more important than maternity, although it cannot, like the latter, be established by the evidence of senses, and that for that reason the child should bear his father's name and be his heir. (Freud, 1939a, pp. 117–118)

Art

In a number of writings, Freud deals with art, at times from a collective perspective—as an institution, an "intermediary realm"—the intersubjective and social effects of artistic works on the receiving public for which it is destined, at times from an individual perspective, that of the artist, of the sources, and of the creative processes. Psychoanalysis provides some answers to certain questions, but is not competent to answer those about the capacities and gifts of artistic creation, such as what emerges from aesthetic techniques, he explained.

I shall present some of his reflections using certain selected texts that seem to me to be of significance and mark certain stages of his work.

So, let me begin with "Formulations on the two principles of mental functioning", in which Freud presents art as being a path, as individual as it is collective, psychic, and socio-cultural, enabling "reconciliation between the two principles", those of pleasure and of reality. Indeed, Freud reminds us that the "realm of phantasy" is a "reserve" fitted out and withdrawn from the requirements of being tested by reality during the development of the sense of reality—that painfully experienced transition from the pleasure principle towards the reality principle—so as to permit a substitute for the gratification of instincts that has to be renounced in actual reality. And artists, like neurotics, have not only withdrawn from the world of this unsatisfying reality, but have also taken refuge in that world of phantasy, giving free rein to their ambitious and erotic wishes. However, thanks to their abilities to *mould their phantasies*, they find their way back to reality through their creations, "truths of a new kind" (Freud, 1911b, p. 224), substitutions procuring fantasised satisfaction of unconscious wishes and then involving the participation of other people, because they can bring to life and satisfy similar unconscious wishes in them.

Thus the artist succeeds where the neurotic fails. In this text, Freud indicated right from the beginning—through art and that back and forth between the "world of phantasy" and reality, underlain by special gifts and sublimational capacities—one of the aspects and one of the major functions, as psychic as it is social, of socio-cultural institutions.

Let us now look at the collective and institutional dimension of art

Artistic creation and enjoyment are part of the "complicated edifice of human wish compensations".

In "The claims of psycho-analysis to scientific interest" (Freud, 1913j), Freud discussed the *instinctual and conflictual foundations* of art and institutions such as neurosis. Then, he presented art as "an intermediate realm" between reality, which refuses to countenance wishes, and the world of phantasy, which realises them. Thanks to "artistic illusion", symbols and substitute formations can cause genuine affects. In addition, it is a matter of a reality that has preserved the child's omnipotence of thoughts and desires. But a reality "allotted by convention" and choice of words points to the institutionalised, social nature of these desires expecting substitutive fantasised satisfaction, something of course suggestive of the Winnicottian notion of intermediate area of play and illusion within which art and religion and, more generally, culture are situated.

In *Totem and Taboo* (1912–1913), Freud invited readers to establish analogies or "striking and far-reaching points of agreement" between neuroses and "those great social institutions art, religion and philosophy", of which, however, they are "distortions". As Paul-Laurent Assoun noted well in *Freud et les sciences sociales* (Assoun, 1993), for Freud, neurosis would remain an "operator of interpretation" and understanding of the socio-cultural field, of its processes and institutions. The only field in which the "omnipotence of thoughts" has been retained in our culture, Freud affirmed, is that of art.

In *The Future of an Illusion*, Freud put artistic creations as a whole alongside the store of ideals and the superego as the "mental assets" of a culture. Even if the satisfaction provided by art generally remains inaccessible "to the masses, who are engaged in exhausting work and have not enjoyed any personal education", it nonetheless offers substitutive satisfactions for the oldest cultural renunciations and thus reconciles people to the sacrifices made for culture. Moreover, by affording an opportunity to share collectively, artistic creations ignite the feelings of identification that every culture needs and generate narcissistic satisfaction when they belong to the accomplishments and heritage of a particular culture, thus evoking its ideals (Freud, 1927c, p. 14).

Analogies may be drawn with certain ideas of Durkheim, notably regarding the preconditions of the creation of a "collective conscience", of a collective reality aiming at the constitution of a group, in particular through religion, its beliefs, representations, and ritual practices. All that presupposes libidinal ties among its members and the forming of a common ideal.

Then in *Civilization and Its Discontents* (Freud, 1930a), the fantasised substitutive satisfactions—offered, in particular, by art, which Freud placed at the head of the list—figure among the "palliative measures", the "defence mechanisms against suffering" helping the human community endure the pain of life. In contrast to reality, they are psychically effective illusions grounded in the "life of the imagination" that are embodied in the artist's creations. They provide fantasised satisfactions, sources of pleasure, but also of consolation in life. They proceed from our mental apparatus' ability to displace the libido from its original instinctual aims, notably through sublimation. The quality of this satisfaction will have to be "characterized meta-psychologically" later on. However, Freud considered that this method of defence was unfortunately not accessible to most people.

Finally, in *New Introductory Lectures* (Freud, 1933a), Freud reminded readers of the harmlessness and beneficence of art and its illusionary nature, free of any danger of encroaching on the world of reality, unlike religion, the eternal enemy of his faith in scientific reason.

At the individual level, a distinction must be made among artists, their activity, their creations and the public, spectators–listeners, readers, forming a unified entity.

Artists

We have already looked at the psychic analogies and social differences between artists and neurotics through their rejection of the world of reality and their withdrawal into the realm of phantasy. While through their creations, artists find their way back to social reality, neurotics, for their part, isolate themselves through their asocial symptomatic formations.

Freud already examined artistic creation through creative writing, its sources, its processes, its means of expression in "Delusions and dreams in Jensen's *Gradiva*" (Freud, 1907a). Creative writers create a "world of phantasy", the very first bits of which are found in children at play. So, what material, what impressions and memories, do creative writers use to *fashion* their work? What paths lead from impulsion, from the imaginativeness of unconscious wishing, to realisation in a work of art? And by means of what processes do they bring this material into their works?

Little by little, Freud recognised the ubiquity of the Oedipus complex, notably in creative writing, in which creative writers choose to present the reasons behind the oedipal state-of-affairs by transforming, modifying, and softening this material through universal literature. For that, he principally referred to Otto Rank's work, *The Incest Theme in Literature and Legend* (Rank, 1912).

Creative writing

In "Creative Writers and Day-Dreaming" (1908e), Freud distinguished between kinds of creative writing, psychological novels—in which, through self-observation, writers split up their egos into many part-egos and personify the conflicting currents of their own inner worlds in their several heroes—and the works refashioning "ready-made and familiar material" "derived from a popular treasure-house of myths, legends and fairy tales". There, the writer retains a certain degree of independence that may express itself both in the choice of material and in the often quite extensive changes in it (Freud, 1908e, pp. 149–152).

Now, wherein does the essential *ars poetica* lie?

For Freud, it lies in "the technique of overcoming the feeling of repulsion" that one may have towards anyone's daydreams and that is inherent in the "barriers that arise between each single ego and the others". This technique uses two specific methods: first, creative writers soften the selfishness of their daydreams by making some formal changes that awaken in us an initial yield of pleasure, or *fore-pleasure*, aesthetic in nature, which will make "possible the release of still greater pleasure or enjoyment arising from deeper psychical sources" and "proceeding from a liberation of tensions in our minds". Once again, a process of identification is at work between the readers–listeners and the creative writer's disguised phantasies (Freud, 1908e, pp. 152–153).

Reception by the public

Works of artists presented to others liberate the same inhibited wishes. Their creation presents the artists' own personal wish-phantasies to others as being realised, but refashioned, therefore disguised and respecting certain aesthetic techniques that procure "incentive pleasure bonuses". According to Freud, artistic enjoyment therefore presents this manifest, formal part and a latent part deriving from the "hidden sources of instinctual liberation" (Freud, 1908e, pp. 152–153).

Another source of artistic enjoyment would be the painful impressions communicated to the spectator of a tragedy, for example, he wrote,

> This is convincing proof that, even under the dominance of the pleasure principle, there are ways and means enough of making what is in itself unpleasurable into a subject to be recollected and worked over in the mind. The consideration of these cases and situations, which have a yield of pleasure as their final outcome, should be undertaken by some system of aesthetics with an economic approach to its subject-matter. (Freud, 1920g, p. 17)

In his work, "Psychopathic characters on the stage" (Freud, 1942a), Freud, in fact, gave thought to dramatic spectacles and how they open up sources of pleasure or enjoyment in spectators–readers. He drew an analogy between being present as a spectator at a play or spectacle as an adult and children at play, which is focused on the painfully suppressed, then displaced, desire to be a hero in contrast to their everyday realities. And the "writer–actor" pair in drama makes that possible by allowing it to *identify* with a hero in a situation of psychic security, as well as sparing it the pain, suffering, and fear that would cancel out its enjoyment. Freud observed that those are preconditions for enjoyment common to several forms of fiction, among them lyric poetry, epic poetry—which allows one to participate in the hero's victories—drama, and all the kinds of suffering and misfortune from which it promises to procure pleasure for spectators, provided that it does not cause them suffering, which is the "first precondition of this form of art". Apart from the enjoyment procured, Freud cited another, the capacity for mental activity aroused. But, drama needs action through which such mental suffering flows and therefore begins with it. This must be action involving conflict and "must include an effort of the will together with resistance". He would identify a certain number of these characterising the type of drama (Freud, 1942a, pp. 305–308). Then in "Thoughts for the times on war and death", he concluded that, "it is an inevitable result of all this that we should seek in the world of fiction, in literature and in the theatre, compensation for what has been lost in life" (Freud, 1915b, p. 291).

Freud also dealt with wittiness, the comical and humour, especially in *Jokes and their Relation to the Unconscious* (Freud, 1905c). Having already explored this theme in my book *Laughter* (Smadja, 1993), I invite readers who are curious and desirous to consult that work.

Before taking leave of the domain of art, I shall discuss notions of aesthetics, beauty and the beautiful that have occupied such an important place in both the life of individuals and that of societies past and present.

It is in *Three Essays on the Theory of Sexuality* (Freud, 1905d) that we first find Freud reflecting on the beautiful and beauty with regard to the excitation aroused by the sight of the sexual object, its genitalia, then, after redirection of sexual curiosity, *sublimation* on to the artistic field through its bodily forms. Then we discover in the course of Freud's writings the astonishing expression "ethical and aesthetic standards of a person's personality or ego", which determine the repression of "bad", selfish, cruel, and sexual behaviour, in particular.

Indeed, associating the adjectives ethical and aesthetic raises questions. Is there some kinship between the good and the beautiful?

In *Civilization and Its Discontents*, Freud raised questions about the "cultural necessity" of beauty and its objects of enjoyment, which does not appear to be obvious, but whose absence is inconceivable. It is a matter of an "aesthetic attitude" offering little protection against the diverse threatening forms of suffering, but, nevertheless, seeming to be able to procure members of a society some compensation for many sacrifices. As for the nature of beauty and of this form of enjoyment, just as in the *Three Essays on the Theory of Sexuality*, he saw it as derived from "the field of sexual feeling", a perfect representative of an aim-inhibited impulse. " 'Beauty' and 'attraction' ", he wrote, "are originally attributes of the sexual object" (Freud, 1930a, p. 83).

If we also consider rather "useless" human accomplishments as being "cultural" in nature, then those pertaining to beauty figure among them and are to be referred to as cultural in nature, for instance, when

> the green spaces necessary in towns as playgrounds and as reservoirs of fresh air are also laid out with flower-beds, or if the windows of the houses are decorated with pots of flowers. We soon observe that this useless thing which we expect civilization to value is beauty. (Freud, 1930a, p. 92)

Finally, this "cultural" significance accorded to beauty is once again emphasised with regard to the aesthetic degradation inflicted by war, participating in our revolt.

Now we have arrived at the end of our exploration of culture as Freud reconstructed it, explored it, and made it intelligible, in particular, with its interconnected, therefore, interdependent institutions. The time has come to present the principal sociologists and anthropologists who were Freud's contemporaries, their own conceptions of society and culture, and to voice certain criticisms of this Freudian discourse.

CHAPTER FOUR

Ideas and criticisms of sociologists and anthropologists

I n the first part of this chapter, I shall discuss the principal representatives of sociology and anthropology among Freud's contemporaries, the majority of them, unfortunately, not well known, even not known at all, by him, something that led him to develop original, personal socio-anthropological ideas based on his psychoanalytical theoretical corpus and taking neurosis and dreams as a model. In the second part, I shall explore certain themes and issues Freud dealt with, which, along with certain sociologists and anthropologists, I shall criticise. Among these themes and issues figure his portrayal of the relationships between the individual and society, his evolutionary thought, symbolism, the idea of group mind. Finally, I shall question his inattention to language, another major social institution.

The sociologist and anthropologist Roger Bastide (Bastide, 1950) proposed identifying two parts in Freud's work: *a social psychology*, which is confused with individual psychology, and *a psychoanalytical sociology* based on instincts, Eros and instincts of destruction, the vicissitudes of their modes of fusion-defusion but also on the transformations of Eros. Freud's psychoanalytical sociology does not take into account the work done in sociology in his time, such as that of the founding fathers, Emile Durkheim and Max Weber. So, his work constitutes a personal reflection on social matters.

In his time, the individual and society were thought to be distinct, antagonistic entities, as were the two separate worlds that constituted the individualistic psychology of the end of the nineteenth century (German, especially, with experimental psychology, and French, with the pathological psychology of Ribot, Janet, and Dumas) and the objectivist sociology of Durkheim.

Based on this conflict between individual and society, his portrayal of the relationship between individuals and society is, therefore, in many respects, in keeping with the social theory of his times. I shall come back to this, but beforehand, let me present the sociology and anthropology of his time through some conceptions of society and culture elaborated by the principal representatives of the fields.

Sociology and anthropology in Freud's time

Sociology

The sociologist Claude Giraud has observed that what seems common to those theorising about sociology at the end of the nineteenth century is that their works present the two sides of an investigation corresponding to a set of problems and objects, coupled with epistemological reflection brought to fruition (Giraud, 1997, p. 41). This was case of Emile Durkheim and Max Weber, the two founding fathers of the field, some of whose major ideas about social phenomena I shall present.

In Germany

Besides Max Weber, I shall point to the presence and roles of Georg Simmel and Ferdinand Tönnies.

Max Weber (1864–1920) and the sociology of action

Let me state, beforehand, that two major thinkers, Karl Marx and Friedrich Nietzsche, shaped Weber's thought. In Weber, a philosophy of struggle and power of Marxist and Nietzschean inspiration combined with the vision of a universal history culminating in a disenchanted world and a subjugated humanity stripped of its loftiest virtues. He considered religions and political ideologies to be illusions.

It was in *Economy and Society: An Outline of Interpretive Sociology* (1922), a treatise on general sociology, that Weber developed an economic sociology, a juridical sociology, a political sociology, and a religious sociology.

According to Weber, sociology is the science of social action, which it wishes to understand through interpretation, and whose unfolding it wishes to explain in social terms—*understand*, that is, to grasp its meanings, *interpret*, that is, to organise the subjective meaning into concepts, and *explain*, that is, to expose the behaviour patterns.

He defined social action as being a form of human behaviour, in other words, an inward or overt attitude oriented towards action or inaction. This behaviour is action when agents attach a certain meaning to their behaviour. Action is social when it takes into account the behaviour of other people in accordance with the meaning the agent confers upon it. Weber then distinguished between four types of actions: goal-instrumental actions; value-rational actions; affectional or emotional actions; and traditional actions.

In addition, social action organises into social relationships when, several agents acting, the meaning of each of their actions takes into account the attitude of the others in such a way that the actions are reciprocally oriented toward one another, thus producing social interactions. The regularity of certain types of social relationships is defined by customs and usage.

He introduced the concepts of legitimate order, said to be conventional and legal, and from there moved on to the concept of struggle. According to him, societies are not actually harmonious wholes. They are made up of struggles as much as of harmonious relationships. Struggle is a basic social relationship. These two concepts enable one, at a subsequent stage of conceptualisation, to move on to the very constitution of social groups. The actors' process of integration may lead to creating either a community or a society. Two other concepts are introduced, those of association and of institution. I shall now discuss the important ones of power and domination.

The difference between power and domination is that in the first case, the commands are not necessarily legal, nor is submission necessarily a duty, while, in the second case, obedience is based on recognition by those who obey the command they are given. The motives behind obedience will therefore enable one to develop a typology of domination. To go from power and domination to political reality, one must add the idea of political community, which contains the ideas of territory, of continuity of community, and of threat of application of physical force to impose respect for the orders or rules. Among these political communities, the State is the authority enjoying the monopoly on physical coercion.

Weber advocated solidarity between the sociological and historical sciences and their correlative causalities. Sociologists do not confine themselves to making the belief systems and behaviours of collectivities intelligible. They wish to ascertain how things have happened, how a certain way of believing determines a certain way of acting, how a certain political organisation influences the organisation of the economy. Causal research would therefore be oriented in two directions, those of historical causality and sociological causality. The former determines the unique circumstances that brought about a certain event. The latter presupposes the establishment of a regular relationship between two phenomena. Weber conceived of causal relations in sociology as being non-comprehensive, probable, partial, without any necessary determinism. This conception of partial intelligibility, moreover, explains Weber's considering that science can only ground incomplete, objective knowledge. This theory of science is indissociable from the ideas about issues facing modernity centred on western capitalistic Europe that he developed. According to Giraud, Weber extracted two main lines of research from this, on the one hand, that of a relationship between a religion—Protestantism—and a mode of economic development—capitalism—and, on the other, that of the rationalisation of the western world and of the consequences of the disenchantment of the world. Science partakes of this extremely broad process of rationalisation since it embraces State and bureaucracy as well as work and economic exchanges or scientific activity (Giraud, 1997, p. 50).

In France

Besides Emile Durkheim, Marcel Mauss (1872–1950) played a considerable role, both in the development of sociology and in French anthropology, and especially in the birth of an anthropology of symbolism that would be expanded upon by Claude Levi-Strauss through his elaboration of structuralism, the other source of which is represented by contributions from the field of linguistics; phonology, in particular. So, I shall recall Mauss's ideas on the question of symbolism, but also on the critique of evolutionism.

Emile Durkheim (1858–1917) and the sociology of social facts

According to Durkheim, society is not a mere aggregate of individuals, but a *system* formed through their association and representing a specific reality endowed with its own characteristics.

It also constitutes an ensemble of more or less interdependent institutions. This functionalist principle of the interdependency of social facts, institutions, and functions became a sociological postulate upon which the sociological method would be based.

The social order emerged as a distinct order arising from nature while transcending it in every direction, but also as a new realm with a complexity of its own. Like all other facts, it was therefore subject to determinism, something that aligned sociology with the natural sciences. The Durkheimian model, therefore, tends to treat social systems as natural realities conforming to organic models, taking an interest in processes, looking for laws, and demonstrating necessary relationships among social activities in search of explanations.

In this way, Durkheim elaborated a doctrine of social facts that highlighted a certain number of criteria (exteriority, obligation or constraint, and specificity) enabling one to recognise the social nature of certain facts, therefore, to distinguish them from other (physical or psychic) facts, the study of which falls within the purview of the natural sciences or psychology.

Social facts are complex because they are syntheses associating individuals and groups, but also ideas and affects. Since social reality is a prolongation of living reality, social facts have come to be "second nature". They function spontaneously. This criterion of spontaneity is a sign of the unconscious dimension of social facts. The holist nature of social phenomena may be associated with it in the sense that society is prior to the individual, or in the sense that each society is a whole—something that implies that a certain coherency of the whole is essential to its components—or, finally, in the sense that since a society is a whole, the whole develops new properties that are not the sum of the qualities of the individuals composing it. This third sense is clearly expressed in organic metaphors consistent with Durkheim's functionalism.

In *Rules of Sociological Method,* Durkheim considered that one must "treat social facts as things" (Durkheim, 1895, pp. 32, 35, 60), meaning as external facts that can be studied objectively, as the other sciences do, and obvious to observation, facts to which we therefore can apply a "method of observation" and analysis (that of the analysis of relationships of causality applied in *Suicide, a Study in Sociology* (Durkheim, 1897)), enabling one to take a step back and observe. These facts exert pressure on individuals and can only be caused by other social facts and never by facts of individual psychology.

This is a two-sided anti-reductionist rule, directed against biologising or racialist/racist reduction as well psychological reductions. Its application enables one to highlight the irreducible complexity of social facts.

Durkheim's sociology therefore had to lay down rules of discrimination in order to distinguish among feelings, ideas, and representations those that are individual and those that are collective. The dividing line founding his entire approach was thus the distribution of labour between psychology and sociology.

Another theme central to his thought is that of the relationship between individuals and the collectivity. How can a collection of individuals constitute a society? How can they arrive at that condition of social existence that is a consensus?

That was the subject of his first book *The Division of Labour in Society* (Durkheim, 1893). He answered that basic question by distinguishing between two forms of solidarity: a form said to be mechanical, with interchangeability of individuals, specific to traditional societies, and a form said to be organic, with differentiation of individuals, characteristic of modern western society.

In Durkheim, the term society, in fact, *has many meanings,* for society is a "laminated" reality. It has several layers, some visible, others hidden, none of which is simple in itself. There is social morphology (volume, density, territorial organisation), social physiology (organisation into clans, tribes, and so on, and the main functions when they are differentiated, i.e., economy, politics), collective representations (values, ideals, myths, and so on).

The core of religion and of social reality is composed of collective representations, meaning of psychic states of specific intensity, but "inner" states all the same, involving mental and affective elements. The representations are forms imposed on things they take hold of and transform. This approach led to the evaluation of the specificity of collective psychic activity, basis of culture and society, and irreducible to any other order. The "collective consciousness" is found in all societies. It is organised and it is through its intermediary that people organise their world view.

As for the notion of culture, which is neither central nor operational in Durkheim's thought, his close collaboration with Mauss all the same made a decisive contribution to the analysis of living cultures and to the construction of the notion of culture through their insistence upon the specificity of each culture, upon its interplay, both necessary and arbitrary, with human universality, upon its internal complexity, upon the role played there by representations, values, and ideals. Yet, as they were discovering elements of a brand new theory, this theory created difficulties for their initial concept of society. They ran up against a dilemma that the human sciences have not totally resolved, namely, that society conditions, limits, and produces that collective, therefore social, creation which is culture. But culture transcends society, works on it from inside, transforms it, makes it more complex, and finally conditions it as well. However, Durkheim, and at times Mauss, tended to make the concept of society more complex so that it could still embrace cultural facts.

Durkheim advocated a conception of history that recognises that human beings do not direct it consciously and often do so without realising it. His conception resulted from the work of historians who had long noticed that events are responses to causes that elude the actors.

According to the sociologist Camille Tarot (Tarot, 1999), Durkheim brought about two revolutions. The first was that it was necessary to study social facts as things, therefore, to found sociology as an empirical science along the lines of the natural sciences; the second was to place symbolism back at the centre of human realities, of social realities, but he did not draw the consequences of that, something that Mauss would do.

Anthropology

The anthropologist Mondher Kilani (Kilani, 2009) argues that it was with the asserting of evolutionist ideas in the domain of science, a reflection on men and women, their society, their evolution, fully becoming an object of science, and the acceleration of the colonial process towards the end of the nineteenth century that anthropology would establish itself as an autonomous scientific field of knowledge, with its methods, its concepts, its "fieldwork", its research and teaching institutions, and its academic and professional sanctions. Nevertheless, it is important to emphasise the transition from the notion of "race" to that of "culture" with the advent of this new science, evolutionist of course, but breaking free of the strict physical determinism that prevailed at the very beginning of the constitution of anthropological knowledge with the craniology of Paul Broca (Broca, 1871), as I have already mentioned with regard to the subject of the notion of culture.

From the second half of the nineteenth century up until around 1910–1920, the evolutionist schools dominated anthropological reflection. Unilinear evolutionism was but the consequence of the whole development of the century's ideas. In a sense it was a reflection of the faith in the continuous progress of humanity, the most fully realised stage of which would be represented by European society of the time. This anthropology provided scientific endorsement for ideological discourse aiming to justify the "need" for colonisation, even its "rationality". This anthropological project, as Kilani has identified particularly well (Kilani, 2009), was therefore born out of the twofold transformation of history into evolution and of alterity into historical difference. The human differences would therefore be historical differences of development understood in terms of backwardness or some deficiency, and the Others are what we were, with western culture serving as the benchmark.

I now want to take a look at the two founders of anthropology: the American anthropologist Lewis Henry Morgan and the British anthropologist Edward Burnett Tylor

Lewis Henry Morgan (1818–1880)

Morgan published two major works: *Systems of Consanguinity and Affinity of the Human Family* (1871) and *Ancient Society* (1877). He gave anthropology one of its objects, kinship, the field that has become classic, a method adapted to this object, the genealogical questionnaire, and some initial scientific results, namely, the discovery of one of the principles that non-European societies had chosen to use to organise ancestral ties and marriage bonds among individuals and the groups composing them, the description of kinship systems. Morgan distinguished among societies in terms of the structuring of kinship. He hypothesised that primitive societies were organised on the basis of kinship, as opposed to more modern societies organised on a political basis. In *Ancient Society* (1877), he proposed to retrace the history of the evolution of humanity on the basis of the evolution of kinship systems. To describe it, he proposed a sequence of three stages or periods: "savagery", "barbarism", and "civilization".

Edward Burnett Tylor (1832–1917)

Unlike Morgan, Tylor was not interested in the development of modes of social organisation. In the opening definition of *Primitive Culture* (1871), he adopted the German concept *Kultur*, for which every culture is a specific unit closed in upon itself, singular, a "complex whole which includes knowledge, belief, art, morals, law, custom, and any other capabilities and habits acquired by man as a member of society" (Tylor, 1871, p. 1).

Culture or civilisation is not considered to be an ideal, but it is a fact that can be observed or reconstituted through the study of the endeavours and major achievements in terms of which it is appropriate to understand it. It is not the end towards which humanity must head, but is first of all tied to a particular society as its own possession. And that is why, in spite of the diverse ways in which it manifests itself, a culture is a whole.

In opposition to religions and the romantics, from the time of *Primitive Culture* (Tylor, 1871), he strove to show that not everything was given in the beginning, but had to be invented, found, diffused. In opposition to "biologists", he strove to show that race explains nothing about cultural facts.

His project and method were basically those of a historian working from the perspective of universal history, the unifying explanatory principle of which was sought for in basic psychology with rationalist and spiritualist leanings.

He, in fact, considered that there was only one human society and therefore only one psychology, but at different stages. How was one to write the history of this thing for which there were no documents? The answer was by creating indirect documents. One can constitute cultural objects without history recorded in historical documents. They must be described, classified, put in order, in terms of their similarities, and then one must ask oneself the famous question at the heart of Tylor's ethnology: invention or diffusion? If the similarity falls under diffusion, one must continue to inquire into the object's cultural history; if it falls under invention, ethnography must turn to psychology to explain the creations of the human mind by the laws of its functioning. By applying the method of indirect evidence to mores and to social facts, one treats them as relics, a concept central to Tylor's thought. Applied to human beings, this notion produces primitives and through them, one can understand something about human ancestorship. They have a civilisation that simply contains the bases of civilisation, ours, and they have finally invented it, for one finds all the basic laws of thought in them.

During the period in which *Totem and Taboo* was published in New York (1918), then in London (1919), unilinear evolutionism, which had prevailed up until the beginning of the twentieth century, was in distinct decline, while new schools of thought, such as diffusionism and functionalism, flourished in Europe and culturalism in the US (Boas and Kroeber, in particular).

Thus, the diffusionist movement, or what is called the cultural history approach, principally led by German anthropo-geographers, was born in reaction to the idea of the unilinear development of societies. It assumed that the process of cultural development is not uniform, but experiences variations resulting from more or less accidental contacts between societies. This idea of multi-variability or multi-evolution is interesting inasmuch as it introduced the idea of the complex and of multiple causality into the development of socio-cultural institutions. Among its representatives are Friedrich Ratzel, Leo Frobenius, and Fritz Graebner.

At the same time, more and more specialised researchers (holding degrees in sociology and anthropology) were leaving to work in the field. There were two periods in this process.

In the early stages, researchers who were not professional ethnographers organised *survey* expeditions fairly rapidly covering an extensive geographical zone. William Halse Rivers Rivers and Charles Gabriel Seligman, both medical doctors by training, were the dominant figures in this first phase. Alfred Cort Haddon thus organised an initial expedition to the Straits of Torres between 1898 and 1899.

Encouraged by Rivers and Haddon, Alfred Reginald Radcliffe-Brown (1881–1955), who graduated from Trinity College, Cambridge (BA, 1905; MA, 1919) in the moral sciences tripos, undertook his initial field work in the Andaman Islands from 1906 to 1908. Then, he spent time in Western Australia from 1910 to 1913. He then published two monographs, *The Andaman Islanders* (1922) and *The Social Organization of Australian Tribes* (1931).

During the second period, starting in the 1920s, the need for intensive ethnographic experience, involving extended stays, language learning, and "participant observation", in particular, were necessary prerequisites for any legitimate theorisation. Thus, the two works epitomising this new regime of "ethnographic authority" were published simultaneously, that of Alfred Radcliffe-Brown (1922), mentioned above and, above all, *The Argonauts of the Western Pacific* by Bronislaw Malinowski (1922). It should be said already at this point that Malinowski in Great Britain and Franz Boas in the US were to be the originators of the new anthropology promulgating the model of ethnographic authority as one of the principal foundations of the new "regime of truth" of contemporary anthropology.

It is to be stressed that the vistas Malinowski opened up, and which would include what was later called functionalism, resulted, on the one hand, from the disappearance of all interest in the historical reconstruction of past societies in terms of linear evolution, and, on the other hand, from the urgent need to investigate the present by taking into consideration the uniqueness and specificity of each culture studied. Indeed, the "autonomy" and "specificity" of each cultural configuration was set down as a primordial requirement of anthropological investigation. Furthermore, Malinowski drew part of his theoretical inspiration from the French sociological school. Durkheim's work led him to discover a basic element that would be at the origin of his scientific "revolution", the importance of sociological "context" in the explanation of social facts. Instead of explaining society just in terms of the history or influence of other cultures, from then on, it would be a matter of finding the explanation in the society itself, in other words, in its "structural and functional consistency", hence the twofold perspective evident in Malinowski's thought. On the one hand, he tried to provide a comprehensive explanation of humanness and human culture in all their dimensions and, on the other, he was attentive to the uniqueness and specific nature of each culture, even if that meant setting out in search of more general and universal laws at a later point.

I have now come to the end of my general presentation of sociology and anthropology contemporaneous with Freud's theoretical elaborations on society and culture.

His depiction of society, culture and the relations between individuals and society or individuals and culture

Depiction of society and culture

To begin with, let us recall that Freud often treated culture and society, even group and community, interchangeably, without caring to distinguish between them. Moreover, that culture or society does not seem to be very differentiated, stratified, and hierarchical, apart from the lower "social classes", the masses, and a ruling minority, which must, however, be educated and furthered.

He wrote of the need for people to cooperate in working to dominate nature and obtain the necessities of life, therefore of a community of interests, and of the need to "regulate social relationships", especially when it came to distributing those necessities of life, but also with an eye to protecting against the dangers of expressing the human instinct of aggressiveness, hence the need to create means of neutralising it through diverse social bonds. *Consequently, he scarcely reflected upon the complexity of the social organisation and social relationships* that sociologists and anthropologists term differentiated social relationships (kinship, economic, political, religious relationships, for example). More fundamentally, *he did not conceive of the phenomenon of emergence* for which, while individuals interacting among themselves in diverse ways constitute society, this *new, social reality* is not similar to the elements constituting it, but possesses properties and characteristics that are indeed new, in its organisation as well as in its processes of functioning and its creations. It forms a *system*, Durkheim maintained, constituted by their association, which therefore represents a unique reality.

However, as I shall demonstrate, *after the fashion of developmentalist theoreticians such as Auguste Comte, Freud ceaselessly compared culture, society to individuals, socio-cultural development to individual development, phylogenesis, and ontogenesis.*

Nonetheless, Paul-Laurent Assoun (Assoun, 1993) has invited us to understand this Freudian approach as part, first of all, of the tradition of Wilhelm Wundt's *Völkerpsychologie* (1912), then of that of British anthropology. For Wundt, this collective psychology represented an "extension" of individual psychology, more than an "application", as it would be for Freud. Within the evolutionist frame of reference of a theory of the human mind's evolution, Wundt especially attempted to discover the causes of the development of the collective psyche, of which the different cultures are but a diversified form, and during the first half of the twentieth century, Freud pursued this approach by reaffirming the interest of a theory of the collective psyche. This "application operation" was itself based on two principles. The first was the comparison of the individual's childhood with the prehistory of peoples and the origin of their institutions, in particular, grounding the transfer of one experience in the other, while the second principle consisted of interpreting and expressing socio-cultural reality through the "individual" language of symptom and neurosis. Consequently, along with Assoun, we may consider that, in order to differentiate itself from it, the Freudian individualising depiction of society and culture also fits into Wundt's epistemological framework and that of his *Völkerpsychologie*.

Paradoxically, in his second topic, Freud would conceive of the individual as a micro-sociological universe. That is what one of his very observant readers, the sociologist Norbert Elias, found. He has written of how Freud conceived of an eminently sociological model of the individual and an eminently individualistic model of society, something that for Elias becomes clearly evident upon examination of the concept of the primal father, who obviously personifies the entire group and social functions as a whole, but in so doing assumes the characteristics of an individual person relatively devoid of structure. However, Elias considers that in Freud's thought, the individual appears as a multipolar complex, a miniature society, compartmentalised into the we, the father, the mother, and so on (Elias, 1990, pp. 136–137).

The individual–society conflict

This depiction of a conflict between individuals and society correlates with other cultural characteristics of Freud's time, such as a certain conception of civilised people as "homo clausus", separated from the social world, the emergence of a consciousness of oneself as separate from others and society, of a personality structure or "social habitus" for which the "I-we" balance accords priority to the "I", as well as of the concept of individual. I would also like to say that it fits into the framework of a liberal bourgeois conception of individuals that prevailed in Viennese society in those days and that Freud espoused.

Proposing to historicise this manner of conceiving the existence of these two distinct, conflicting realities, to inquire into the conditions of its surfacing and the stage of its emergence, Elias observed that it resulted from the *civilising process*, but also from the construction of the modern state.

Both individual and collective, this *civilising process* is principally characterised by the transformation of standards of feelings and behaviour, by the internalisation of external constraints into self-constraint, by acquiring mastery over emotions correlative to the formation of a superego, characteristic of the "psychic *habitus*" of all civilised individuals or "personality structure" of "civilized" people, and in a relationship of interdependency and correspondence with the social structures and the sociogenesis of the State.

This process has led to the gradual split between aspects of human life that may find expression in social relationships, therefore are "permitted", and those that must remain private, therefore are "prohibited" in public. Two spheres of each person's life are then differentiated, one private, secret, the other public, overt, something that would have an impact not only on the depiction of relationships between individuals and social reality, but also on the transformation of the psychic structure of human beings, notably along the lines of the creation of inner splits, of an ego, of a repressed part of the psyche, of a superego (Elias, 1939).

The social identity of individuals

Freud did not take into consideration the social identity of individuals either. Nor did he take into account the identity of the "we", the profoundly social nature of the person, or detect the two levels of human existence, the individual level, the "I", and the social level, the "we", which he thought of as two objects strictly separated one from the other while being inextricably mixed together. These two levels conflict with one another and come under two distinct modes of observation.

Freud's evolutionist thought and British anthropology's influence on him: the indirect criticisms of Durkheim and Mauss, via Tylor and Frazer

In his socio-anthropological writings, principally *Totem and Taboo*, Freud especially borrowed from the British evolutionists' system of construction of facts, reconstruction of the past, and interpretation converging with hypotheses of his that he wished to validate, something that kept him from according interest and value to other socio-anthropological schools, namely, to the diffusionism of German anthropo-geographers, the sociological method introduced by Durkheim and Mauss—which would influence Malinowski's functionalism and Radcliffe-Brown's structuro-functionalism—and American culturalism, that of Boas and Kroeber in particular.

Evolutionism, developmentalism, progressivism: preliminary clarifications in conjunction with Camille Tarot and Mondher Kilani

Mondher Kilani has pointed out that by ridding itself of the Christian dogma of origin and predetermination, the eighteenth century introduced the idea of an evolving history of humanity, to the detriment of the idea of an unchanging creation entirely subject to divine will. It brought to light a new category, unrecognised up until then, that of *evolution*. The idea of *repetitive, cyclical time* was therefore abandoned to open the way to a notion of *progressive, linear time*. As a result, eighteenth century people accepted the idea of change and began to apply it to the history of humanity and to that of their own society (Kilani, 2009, p. 203). As part of this same dynamic, the eighteenth century discovered relativity and the historical situating of cultures. In addition, Kilani points to the birth in the nineteenth century, in the wake of the Enlightenment, of a new concept, the human being. Falling, up until that time, under metaphysics, ethics, or partaking of transcendence, human beings therefore became implicated in nature and the social mechanism. From that time on, they perceived themselves to be social objects, actors in history. They became the means of knowing themselves.

For his part, the sociologist Camille Tarot (Tarot, 1999) has detected the existence of several evolutionisms, at least two, in terms of the object, the method, and the era. By extending to prehistory and primitive peoples, socio-cultural evolutionism—the work of philoso-phers (Hume, De Brosses, Condorcet), ideologists, and the first theo-reticians of progress—that appeared during the eighteenth century, preceding by a good century the biological evolutionism correlative to Darwinian theory, served as a *matrix* for the first "ethnologists". According to him, it would be better called *cultural progressivism*. How does he characterise it?

This progressivism, which would also be political, did not consider it sufficient to see that culture or society were on the move and in the making. It wished to shape the course of progress, not only in actual fact, but in theory in order to predict and orient it. Not delimited by any intelligible structure, it was indefinite. From then on, progress naturally became a revolutionary, modern founding myth, but it was also the founding myth that made the human sciences possible as such, something that, as it happens, is to be found in Freudian thought, a product of its times.

However, Tarot has found that the criticisms of nineteenth century anthropological evolutionism do not yet sufficiently distinguish between *cultural progressivism* and *developmentalism*.

Developmentalism, in fact, functions according to the model of the individual who belongs to a genus or a species and whose develop-ment consists of oriented, limited *organic* growth that takes place. So, does a society have a childhood, a period of growth, an adulthood, and a natural end? Comte conceived of an "intellectual" developmen-talism on the scale of all of humanity conceived as a single society with its law of the three states. It was the same for Freud who conceived of society as an individual, thus adopting a *developmentalist* conception, but one he would associate with the liberal bourgeois ideology of progress, therefore, with *socio-cultural progressivism*, as identified and differentiated by Tarot.

Tarot combined Herbert Spencer's conception with these two forms of evolutionism. What would bring these different evolu-tionisms together was not the confused, non-generalisable idea of evolution, Tarot has found, but a mode of explanation, *the idea that the simple explains the complex*.

James G. Frazer and Edward Burnett Tylor espoused one of the forms of evolutionism, the distinctive feature of which was to try to explain cultural changes by human psychology. They wished to write a history that was a prehistory, meaning one for which no written documents were available, something that links up with the Freudian anthropological approach, and that would be hotly contested by Durkheim and Mauss, founders of the sociological method, which was to have to apply to all of the social sciences as a whole, including anthropology.

From the questionable establishment of "evolutionist" facts to the sociological constitution of facts

The principal criticisms applicable to the methodology Freud used— in *Totem and Taboo*, in particular—that I shall present reflect the radical opposition between two schools of thought, the anthropological evolutionism reigning at that time and the emergence of a new method of apprehending socio-cultural reality, Durkheim's and Mauss' sociological method, correlative to the creation of a new social science, sociology, and the French school of sociology, contemporaneous with that of Max Weber, and the creation of psychoanalysis.

The *first criticism* is levelled against the manner of constructing socio-cultural facts (beliefs, institutions, customs, for example) through series of similar facts or superficial similarities *taken out of their social context*, therefore, not connected with the social system of which they are a part, their social dimension, which is consequently not studied in its own right. In so doing, not reaching down into the concrete, complex realities, evolutionism does not come into contact with social reality, and the facts "remain up in the air". However, it is by connecting religious facts, for example, to their social substratum once and for all that one lends them their genuine features, their place. This reproach is particularly addressed to Frazer, and by extension to the Freudian conception of religion. Mangled in this way, the facts only account for one aspect of reality. These ethnographical objects are then fragmentary, something that disrupts societies, which are not studied in and for themselves, but in a piecemeal fashion.

The *second criticism* concerns explanation–interpretation. It is still a matter of tracking down the individual mental processes upon which one believes social facts are based. The discovery of psychological principles exhausts the search and explanation, which is banal and too general. This method is actually still one of the branches of individual psychology. However, one of the rules of this new sociological method consists of explaining social facts by other social facts, and not by appealing to facts and principles falling under this order of psychological reality. It is a matter of singling out the social reality and of differentiating it from psychological reality.

Inspired by the method of historical criticism, Mauss' work began with a *criticism of evidence*. He considered it essential to avail oneself of facts situated well in space and time, which was not the case with the imprecise, even false, insufficiently criticised ethnographical material of his colleagues.

Another of Mauss' criticisms involved tracing history not attested to by any document. Sociology and ethnology do not give anyone the right to compose a fictitious narrative about origins on the basis of some fictional or surmised history or, for that matter, to respond to our historical curiosity by creating a substitute for history that is unsatisfactory for want of documents. Consequently, those fields must be subjected to the discipline of the historico-critical method that would have to prevail in all work in the social sciences from that time on. So it was that Freudian speculations about the phylogenesis of culture would be vehemently rejected.

Mauss also decried the "ethnocentric" carving up facts.

By more or less dealing with all juridical, religious, technological, economic, political, or artistic phenomena, ethnography carves up traditional societies in accordance with classifications in use in the observers' society of origin. Mauss sensed that other definitions of objects, or of these special functions, had to be found, because ethnographic observation showed that, in the reality of the societies observed, meaning in the actual behaviour of the people in general, and a fortiori in primitive societies, everything is given at the same time. He very quickly saw that all human behaviour was comprehensive, that it did not conform to the carving up imposed upon it in the name of psychology or social physiology, but operated synthetically. Therefore, sociology had to revise all the forms of categorisation, and its own to begin with. Mauss was concerned about this problem, which would lead him to the idea of the symbolic nature of social facts.

Let us move on to the criticism of comparison and to the differences between Mauss' and Durkheim's approaches.

Emblematic of French sociology, they opposed that superficial, serial method of doing things, the rule of the one well-studied case, as well as the comparison of well-established facts in keeping with the sociological method. Thus, the comparisons made by the Englishmen were invalidated from the outset because they focused on facts that were too incomplete. One of the most positive contributions made by the sociological method is certainly to have laid down that comparison is only valid if it secures criteria of comparability such as that of similar types of societies to be compared.

Nevertheless, Mauss lamented the fact that, after the fashion of their British colleagues, Durkheim retained only similarities, at the expense of differences, which are just as significant, in particular in studying religions. Why? Because they inform us about placing the facts within their contexts and, consequently, are part of the fact itself. That was his concern to respect the whole, something that Freud did within the field of psychopathology but, much too taken up with his method of crudely transferring from the individual to the collective in search of validation of his hypotheses, he neglected to do in the socio-cultural field.

Complexity and historicity of societies

In addition, Mauss stressed the relativity of the evolutions and above all their distinctness. Societies are realities so complex that no strict consistency prevails between their levels and their components, something to which Freud willingly subscribed when it came to the psyche. One must grasp the relations each time and respect each society's individuality before making comparisons. As a consequence, comparison grows increasingly difficult.

Thus, social facts are complex wholes, bundles of relations, and this has multiple consequences, among them, I shall mention: the end of primitive peoples, an invention of the evolutionists, leading to closing the question about origins, which would thus free one to look for a more discriminating perception of the differences among these people divided up into different peoples; the complexity and historicity of primitive societies invalidating the simplifications of evolutionism or developmentalism; the object of ethnology no longer being about the difference between civilised/non-civilised, but only about the differences of all civilisations among themselves.

Finally, Mauss proposed *constituting* the facts sociologically and, by appealing to tested sociological and historical procedures, connecting them with mankind's psychic depths. He discovered the structure enabling one to connect sociological analysis with these psychic depths. This was the *symbolic* he presented to psychologists and sociologists in his 1924 lecture.

The symbolic, symbolism, symbolisation, and the symbolic nature of social facts: Freud, Durkheim, and Mauss

Common to every individual—normal, dreamer, and neurotic—and to every culture, symbolism enabled Freud, on the one hand, to establish links between individual and collective human realities and, on the other, to accord psychoanalysis, its investigative techniques, and its major concepts, a central and intermediary position in relation to sciences of the mind, those of history and culture. Unfortunately, he did not seem to consider that these sciences of the mind could contribute anything more to psychoanalysis than the elimination of the impression of "strangeness" of individual formations, those of neurotic symptoms or dreams. Finally, though acknowledging that symbolism was part of the activity of the unconscious mind, "especially that of the people", unlike his contemporaries Durkheim and Mauss, Freud did not draw the fundamental, ultimate consequences of this for the understanding of society and culture. Moreover, starting from the instinctual foundations of society and culture, as well as from their formations, such as institutions, he would no longer consider the latter to be symbolic creations, but "social compromise solutions" to the problem of wish compensation, and "mankind's assets".

Tarot (Tarot, 1999) has observed that, through the totem, Durkheim accorded a central place to the problem of symbols in his *Elementary Forms of Religious Life* (Durkheim, 1912), contemporaneous with *Totem and Taboo* (Freud, 1912–1913), but it is found again with respect to rites, assemblies, and "effervescent groups", and it was also at the root of the interest Durkheim never denied having in totemism, which only seemed to him to be the elementary form of religion because he hoped to see the elementary forms of symbolisation in it. He came to formulate the essential idea there that *no society can exist without symbols and that all social life is based on a vast symbolism.* He developed a sociological theory of symbolisation, about the totem, "flag of the clan", place of projection of collective force, then about rites, assemblies, and "effervescent groups". Totemism therefore represented a symbolic fact, and religion became a system of symbols.

Tarot has stressed that in rare passages of *Elementary Forms of Religious Life*, Durkheim came to consider that society and symbolisation went together, that without symbolisation there would be no social order. Hence, one could conclude that society perhaps did not completely pre-exist symbolisation, but creates itself and establishes itself with it. From then on, symbolisation would be the process by which a group in relation with the world creates itself, not only by establishing its representations, but creates them and establishes them by exchanging them in visible forms. Symbols do not, therefore, only serve to express representations and affects or social morphology. They contribute to forming, establishing, and transmitting them.

Moreover, a parallel is to be drawn between the Freudian scenario of the murder of the father of the primal horde, condition of the creation of totemic culture, first phase of the evolution of the so-called human culture, and the scenario-myth of *Elementary Forms of Religious Life* as Tarot analyses it. Durkheim, in fact, also wished to show, through Australian totemism, how one has gone from the primal horde to the clan. And that is archaistic on his part. However, he wished to emphasise that the transition took place through *collective symbolisation*, something applicable to the Freudian scenario. And that is what is new in his thought.

In Mauss' life work (1872–1950), let us note the interaction among sociology, ethnology, history, science of religions, and philology. By practising an interdisciplinary approach, he was able to rethink sociology, the history of religions, and ethnography—and thus transform the doctrine of social facts inherited from Durkheim—to arrive at the "total social fact", consequence of the symbolic nature of social facts.

In his lecture on "The real and practical relationships of psychology and sociology" presented before Société de psychologie in 1924, Mauss told his colleagues that he had discovered the structure within which one could connect the sociological analysis and humanity's psychic depths.

He explained that along with Durkheim, he had long thought that one of the features of the social fact was precisely its symbolic aspect, for in most collective representations, it is not a matter of a single representation of one thing, but of a representation arbitrarily, or more or less arbitrarily, chosen to signify other ones and oblige practices. *The activity of the collective spirit is even more symbolical than that of the individual spirit*, but it is so in exactly the same sense. From this point of view, there is only a difference of intensity, of species, no difference of genus (Mauss, 1950, p. 294).

This notion of symbol that had lately been of concern to psychology had, therefore, completely naturally *mediated* between the two disciplines for Mauss. This new distribution of labour reflected profound changes in the understanding of the facts to be studied. The psychic and the social represent two modalities and two points of view regarding the same human reality of the "total human being" and of the "total social fact". Symbolisation is played and replayed on the interface of all these dimensions. It is, therefore, not the exclusive property of sociologists, but also concerns psychologists and, why not, physiologists.

In his *A General Theory of Magic* (Mauss & Hubert, 1902), written with Henri Hubert, Mauss showed that symbols and signs refer to one another and not only to the things, the referents they designate, constituting in this way "chains", networks called symbolisms (those of a rite, a religion, a culture) and the whole forms the symbolic, an order proper and functionally necessary to the human world. This world of symbolisms is a necessary condition of the existence of every group as such and it represents a new sphere, that culture, social creation, which the human element slips in between nature and itself and that unites them in a new order. So, every culture, every society, is made up of a multiplicity of symbolisms. Social life presupposes them everywhere.

This symbolism is bound to an activity of the human mind, symbolic thought that actively places elements of the world into relationship with one another. Mauss recognised that, underlying all thought, it is the first form of human thought. In addition, he identified the mechanism of producing meaning that is at the heart of social life and that is, in a sense, prior to it. Adopting the term of the English psychologist Henry Head, he called this mechanism *symbolic function*, which Levi-Strauss would later make his own.

Tarot has found that the symbolic in Mauss' sense is not one layer among others, but what explains that social reality (and, undoubtedly, human reality) is made up of several layers, that it is a superimposition of interconnected networks. Moreover, Mauss did not hesitate to posit "translation" relationships between all levels of reality, between the sociological and the psychological, between society and individuals, but also within the sociological itself, between the economic, the social, the political, the religious, the aesthetic, finally between the psychological, the sociological, and the biological.

Thus, everything social is symbolic. Meaning and force flow among all levels of its reality and these levels intertranslate. Everything acts upon everything.

Now, here we have a theoretical conception that Freud might have found enticing had he shown interest in French sociological thought instead of favouring the evolutionist thought of the British anthropologists. Mediating between the psychological and the socio-cultural, he would certainly have replaced the symbolic by the unconscious, which, moreover, he tried to do with his methodological impertinence. However, this perspective remains to be elaborated within a multidisciplinary, collaborative framework.

From that point on, starting with Mauss, then Levi-Strauss, social anthropology would deal with cultures as *symbolic systems*, taking an interest in configurations, seeking out structures, demonstrating the coherence of the phenomena it interpreted.

Group mind and collective consciousness

Freud conceptualised the notion of "group mind" in *Totem and Taboo* as a continuation of Wundt's theory of the collective mind, generative, especially of the "store of ideals" and "cultural super-ego" formulated in *Civilization and Its Discontents*.

This hypothesis—which served Freud as a foundation everywhere, and in which psychic processes take place as in the psychic life of an individual—*grounds the existence of the psychology of peoples, ensures continuity in the emotional life of people over generations*, especially as concerns consciousness of guilt following the collective criminal act of the brothers, which would be perpetuated throughout generations of people who knew nothing of it, but *also conditions all progress and all development, both individual and collective*.

This notion of group or collective mind would be vigorously attacked by Malinowski in his book *Sex and Repression in Savage Society* (1927), just as he would criticise the Durkheimian notion of "collective consciousness" displaying some similarities with the Freudian notion.

Durkheim, in fact, already defined the concept of "collective consciousness" in his first work *Division of Labor in Society* (1893), where he wrote that the "totality of beliefs and sentiments common to the average members of a society forms a determinate system with a life of its own. It can be termed the collective or common consciousness". *This would be the "psychological type" of the society, which "does not change with every generation, but on the contrary, links successive generations to one another"* (Durkheim, 1893, pp. 38–39, my emphasis). This collective consciousness would be widespread or strong in varying degrees, depending on the societies, being more predominant in societies with mechanical solidarity than in those of organic solidarity. More precisely,

> Two consciousnesses exist within us: the one comprises only states that are personal to each one of us, characteristic of us as individuals, whilst the other comprises states that are common to the whole of society. The former represents only our individual personality, which it constitutes; the latter represents the collective type and consequently the society without which it would not exist. (Durkheim, 1893, p. 61)

They are, moreover, interdependent. Nevertheless, he stated in a footnote that since every individual is necessarily part of several groups, there are therefore several collective consciousnesses within us.

Two years later, in *Rules of Sociological Method* (Durkheim, 1895), just as he would draw attention to the specificities of the sociological method pertaining to observation and the analysis of this most singular social reality distinct from biological and psychological realities, he described the collective consciousness that probably would have been of interest to Freud and group psychoanalysts, although its unconscious dimension could not be captured.

He reminded us that social life results from the specific combination of individual consciousnesses and, afterward, it is this combination that explains it. He wrote,

> By aggregating together, by interpenetrating, by fusing together, individuals give birth to a being, psychical if you will, but one which constitutes a psychical individuality of a new kind. Thus it is in the nature of that individuality and not in that of its component elements that we must search for the proximate and determinant causes of the facts produced in it. The group thinks, feels, acts entirely differently from the way its members would if they were isolated. If therefore we begin by studying these members separately, we will understand

nothing about what is taking place in the group. In a word, there is between psychology and sociology the same break in continuity as there is between biology and the physical and chemical sciences. (Durkheim, 1895, p. 129)

Let us now take a look at Malinowski's criticisms of the Freudian notion of "group mind", then of Durkheim's notion of "collective consciousness". Malinowski wrote,

And here we touch upon a very important point: the methodological need of the figment of a collective soul. As a point of fact, no competent anthropologist now makes any such assumption of "mass psyche", or of the inheritance of acquired "psychic dispositions", or of any "psychic continuity" transcending the limits of the individual soul. (Malinowski, 1927, p. 125)

About this, he stated in a footnote that none of the anthropologists Freud drew from, among them Frazer, ever used a concept of this kind in their analyses of beliefs, customs, and institutions. Furthermore, he observed that Durkheim "who verges upon this metaphysical fallacy" (Malinowski, 1927, p. 125), was criticised on this point by most contemporary anthropologists, among them Boas and Kroeber, who themselves avoided it. According to Malinowski,

On the other hand, anthropologists can clearly indicate what the medium is in which the experiences of each generation are deposited and stored up for successive generations. This medium is that body of material objects, traditions, stereotyped mental processes which we call civilization. It is super-individual but not psychological. It is moulded by man and moulds him in turn. It is the only medium in which man can express any creative impulse and thus add his share to the common stock of human values. It is the only reservoir from which the individual can draw when he wants to utilize the experiences of others for his personal benefit. The fuller analysis of culture to which we shall presently pass will reveal to us the mechanism by which it is created, maintained, and transmitted. (Malinowski, 1927, pp. 125–126)

For my part, I consider that this group mind is a component of culture and both its processes and formations present, of course, some analogies with those of the individual psyche, but also its singularities to be identified. It is culture that, in diverse ways, by its functions of transmission of ways of feeling, thought, representations, and practices ensures the continuity between the generations of a society. Culture represents *heredity that is just as social as interpsychical.*

The Freudian inattention to language

Although Freud discussed the question of language and languages—notably with regard to the origin of symbols that could have come from the earliest phases of the evolution of the language and of the formation of concepts, as well as when he brought up the presence of "ambivalent concepts" combining within them antithetical meanings in the "language of dreams", as in the oldest roots of historical languages, according to the hypotheses of linguists such as Karl Abel (1884), to whom he refers in his text "The antithetical meaning of primal words" (Freud, 1910e)—he clearly did not include language, among the primordial institutions within culture and society. Yet, in "The claims of psycho-analysis to scientific interest" (Freud, 1913j), he dealt with the interest of psychoanalysis for linguistics. Of course, even in this passage, he only dealt with the language of dreams, its symbolism, and with the language of symptoms—contrary to what is announced in the title! How are we to understand this setting aside of language?

In particular, he was clearly unaware of the existence of the illustrious linguist of the time, Ferdinand de Saussure in Geneva, and his *Course in General Linguistics*, edited by two of his students Charles Bally and Albert Sechehaye in 1915. However, he probably did have knowledge of Max Müller's works on comparative mythology and historical linguistics. Saussure indeed revolutionised linguistics in his day, approaching language strictly synchronically and no longer diachronically. In the manner of Durkheim's and Mauss' sociological method, he explored language and the facts of language in and for themselves, forming a system. He casts aside the question of origins, which had been of such concern to nineteenth century linguists.

Thus, Saussure would have taught Freud that a language was also a social institution. It is external to speakers and transcends their speech acts, which only actualise part of its potentialities. Since it pre-exists speakers, as society does its members, a language is defined as a deposit, a treasure, conveying tradition. Like other social realities, it imposes itself on its speakers. The facts of languages are marked by obligation, because a language is a body of socially instituted rules. This language has its own order that must be taken into consideration for its own sake if one wishes to bring out the rules governing its functioning. Languages are the most important system of signs, and linguistic signs have a characteristic distinguishing them from symbols, their arbitrariness. As a system, a language is form, not substance, only being made up of relations, of "differences".

A language seems to be a variable dependent on the structure of society. It shifts and adapts itself when society is transformed. One could write a sort of history paralleling variations in the meanings of words and the evolution of society.

The particularity of each language, as of every society, is to be emphasised. It is the thing of a community, as is culture. Language is both general and particular, therefore, general in all the individuals of that community who say the word, speak the language, and consequently think in that way, but it is only common among them.

Through this experience of language, as internal and personal as it is social, and through this science, we grasp the three aspects of language—physiological, psychological, and sociological—which can be analysed separately and in connection with one another.

We have now come to the end of the discussion of some of the criticisms levelled at Freud. Let us now look at the notion of *Kulturarbeit*, which runs through his work and implicitly takes on a central role.

CHAPTER FIVE

The Freudian notion of *Kulturarbeit*

Thoughts about the genealogy and the problems involved in the translation of Kulturarbeit

Kulturarbeit is a word composed of *Kultur* and *Arbeit*. It raises many different kinds of questions for us.

Regarding its structure, which reflects certain linguistic characteristics of the German language

The German language can, in fact, combine, put together, several words to form a single word. Very often the combination of words serves to fine-tune the original words.

What are the principles of composition underlying *Kulturarbeit*?

It is the conjunction of two "genuine" nouns. Somewhat in the manner of an adjective, the first noun, *Kultur* (culture or civilisation, the determiner) qualifies the second noun *Arbeit* (work, determined as the principal term). Nevertheless, Jean Laplanche, the scientific director of the German to French translation of Freud's complete works (Freud, 2010), considers that, depending on the terms under consideration, the notion of "qualifying" has its limitations and the terminology must respond to a twofold concern to detect in a precise way the *relation* or, more often, *relations* existing between the two terms, but also to opt for a translation that preserves the polysemy and sometimes ambiguousness involved in linking them (Laplanche, 1989, p. 59). Thus, depending on the case, he might choose the *adjectival* form (cultural work or cultural activity) or the *definite* form (work of civilisation), for example. However, in most cases Laplanche's translation team chose the adjectival form (cultural work), without ever opting for the definite form.

In *Kulturarbeit*, *Kultur* definitely seems to qualify *"Arbeit"* in response to the question as to what kind of work it is a matter of. But not just that.

Regarding the specifically Freudian language, therefore, his ever evolving thought and work, as well as his sources of inspiration

What, according to Laplanche, as a Freudologist, German scholar, and translator, are its characteristics?

Freud was a remarkable creator of concepts, of a conceptual apparatus, of terms, but also of a linguistic code, a distinctive idiom. And, Freudian usage particularly made use of the linguistic potentialities of the German language.

Laplanche considers that if Freud's ways of conceptualisation are multiple, they practically only had a single origin, namely in linguistic usage, most often in ordinary language, more rarely in the language of other scientific disciplines (Laplanche, 1989, p. 43).

Thus, Laplanche has observed, Freud most particularly engaged in, and excessively so, the fabrication of compound words. There are thousands of them in his language, from the simplest to the most complex, from the most ordinary to the strangest (Laplanche, 1989, p. 45). So it is that Laplanche has identified numerous problems specific to Freud's language involving:

- The fact that certain compound words are found only in Freud.
- The fact that Freud confers a meaning upon certain of these compound nouns that is only found in his works.
- The firm anchorage of the meaning of the compound words employed by Freud within the context of his work.

This is why translating the Freudian concepts expressed by compound words requires very good knowledge both of German and of Freud's thought and work.

Consequently, regarding the difficulties of translating the term,
whether it is a matter of English, but also of French and of
Spanish, in particular

Translating *Kulturarbeit*, in fact, combines the difficulties proper to the
German language and to Freudian language.

The diverse existing translations display all the ambiguity of the
relationship between determiner and what is determined. Only the
context can permit one to come to a decision. *Kulturarbeit* has thus been
translated into English, French, and Spanish in numerous ways.

In addition, my exploration of this Freudian notion has made apparent a
polysemy finding expression in different translations, no matter what the
language.

Correlated with its polysemic nature, this multiplicity of translations was
decisive in my choice to retain the original German term Kulturarbeit.

Is this a matter of a neologism created by Freud, or might he have
borrowed it from ordinary language, or from a writer and an epistemological corpus? Moreover, it is conceivable that he imagined
that he created this compound word, though it already existed in
another field of knowledge. In particular, did it exist in German or
Anglophone anthropology? My research has not unearthed anything of that nature. *Kulturarbeit* did not exist in the anthropological
corpus.

If it was a matter of a Freudian neologism, unknown up until then
in the field of human sciences, it would be interesting to weigh the
issues involved. I plan to examine them.

The German scholars–translators I have consulted, among them
Jean-Claude Capèle, have all hypothesised that in all probability, since
Kulturarbeit did not figure in dictionaries of the German language prior
to 1900, the year of its first occurrence in Freud's work, Freud might well
have created this term. For example, it is to be spotted in the third
edition of the Sachs-Villatte German-French dictionary published in
1906. And, although it might well have existed in Freud's everyday
language, it is also quite probable that he created a *neologism of*
meaning, though not of *form*, something that concurs with my own
hypothesis. Indeed, I consider that within his dynamic of creation of
compound neologisms using the determined *Arbeit*—a central notion
in psychoanalysis, borrowed, not from the socio-economic corpus, but

rather from Hermann von Helmholtz and Gustav Theodor Fechner, both physicists and founders of experimental psychology, who, along with Wilhelm Wundt, influenced and inspired Freud—to which he added the determiner *Kultur*, a Germanic concept created by eighteenth century German bourgeois intellectuals, as I explained before, he produced a particularly *heterogeneous* term.

Kulturarbeit *in Freud's writings*

Introducing the notion

We discover the first occurrence of the notion of *Kulturarbeit* (cultural work; work of civilisation, cultural activity) in *The Interpretation of Dreams*, precisely where Freud deals with the "dream of embarrassment due to nakedness" in the section devoted to typical dreams. Indeed, he writes there of "paradise", "a group fantasy of the childhood of the individual", when human beings were naked and without shame in one another's presence until shame and anguish awoke, expulsion followed, and "sexual life and the tasks of cultural activity began" (Freud, 1900a, p. 245). This cultural activity is to be understood as the realisation, accomplishment, of human "cultural development" in its individual and social dimension, as well as in the life of society.

Then, in " 'Civilized' sexual morality and modern nervousness", Freud used the term five times—undoubtedly as synonymous with cultural activities—associating it from the start with the process of sublimation supplying necessary energy. He wrote that, "civilized sexual morality is a sexual morality obedience to which . . . spurs men on to intense and productive cultural activity" (Freud, 1908d, p. 181). Elsewhere, we find his statement that, "The forces that can be employed for cultural activities are that to a great extent obtained through the suppression of what are known as the perverse elements of sexual excitation" (Freud, 1908d, p. 189). Later on, in "Thoughts for the times on war and death", we discover its appearance as work accomplished collectively, therefore producing a common endeavour,

> Observation showed, to be sure, that embedded in these civilized states there were remnants of certain other peoples, which were universally unpopular and had therefore been only reluctantly, and even so not fully, admitted to participation in the common work of

civilization, for which they had shown themselves suitable enough. (Freud, 1915b, p. 276)

In 1927, in *The Future of an Illusion, Kulturarbeit* is mentioned four times in different acceptations. Indeed, on two occasions, Freud writes there of "coercion in the work of civilization" to which people are subjected (Freud, 1927c, pp. 7–8), then of the "work of civilization", which protects us from feelings of helplessness in face of the superior force and dangers of nature (Freud, 1927c, p. 16), but also of "many thousands of years of the work of civilization" having banished social chaos and established order and the maintenance of human society through the intermediary of religion (Freud, 1927c, p. 34).

The term is found twice in 1930 in *Civilization and Its Discontents*, where Freud wrote that, "The work of civilization has become increasingly the business of men, it confronts them with ever more difficult tasks and compels them to carry out instinctual sublimations of which women are little capable" (Freud, 1930a, p. 103), but also produces the cultural superego expressing its demands via an ethic regulating social relations. Finally, in "Dissection of the psychical personality", Lecture XXXI of the *New Introductory Lectures on Psycho-Analysis*, the "work of culture" would seem analogous to psychoanalytic work and its therapeutic endeavours. For the ego, it is a matter of a work agenda for gradually conquering other pieces of the id, "Where id was, there ego shall be. It is a *work of culture*, not unlike the draining of the Zuider Zee" (Freud, 1933a, Lecture XXXI, p. 80, my emphasis).

In addition, throughout Freud's work, we find numerous allusions, references, implicit, but also explicit, to *Kulturarbeit*, both in his socio-anthropological writings and in other texts. I am thinking, for example, of the notion of "individual culture" acquired during the period of latency in *Three Essays on the Theory of Sexuality* (Freud, 1905d, p. 242); the "susceptibility to culture" resting on the transformation of instincts (Freud, 1915b, pp. 282–284); and "the process by which an individual rises to a comparatively high plane of morality" (Freud, 1915b, p. 281); in "Thoughts for the times on war and death"; the notions of human "cultural development" based on isolating and developing "the archaic, animal heritage of humanity" (Freud, 1919g, p. 262), innate reservoir of instinctual forces; of the process of civilisation ("the changes which it brings about in the familiar instinctual dispositions of human beings") in *Civilization and Its Discontents*

(Freud, 1930a, p. 96); that of "cultural aims" (Freud 1930a, p. 103) of the "organization of the ego" (Freud, 1915c, p. 132); of "the cultural demands of the individual" (Freud, 1933a, Lecture XXXV, p. 181); the "subject's cultural and ethical ideas" (Freud, 1914c, p. 93) (which exercise authority and impose cultural requirements); civilisation as "a necessary course of development from the family to humanity as a whole . . ." (Freud, 1930a, p. 133).

I hypothesise that there is a latent, quasi continual, presence of *Kulturarbeit* just below the surface, both in Freud's writings and in his mind. So, this notion would be something to discover through its multiple contents, processes, functions, and meanings scattered throughout his writings. Let us explore them.

The Interpretation of Dreams (Freud, 1900a)

In *The Interpretation of Dreams*, Freud alludes to the lost paradise of our childhood during which the exhibitionistic pleasure in nakedness was not prohibited, therefore not yet an object of shame, and where feelings of modesty had not yet taken hold in the mind. Shame and feelings of modesty are presented as being acquisitions of the cultural development of all human beings participating in social life. Dreams then preserve the expression of those infantile impulses. But these dreams of nakedness figure among the typical dreams that he identified:

> When we look back at this unashamed period of childhood it seems to us a Paradise; and Paradise itself is no more than a group phantasy of the childhood of the individual. That is why mankind were naked in Paradise and were without shame in one another's presence; till a moment arrived when shame and anxiety awoke, expulsion followed, and sexual life and the *tasks of cultural activity* began. But we can regain this Paradise every night in our dreams. I have already . . . expressed a suspicion that impressions of earliest childhood (that is, from the prehistoric epoch until about the end of the third year of life) strive to achieve reproduction, from their very nature and irrespectively perhaps of their actual content, and that their repetition constitutes the fulfilment of a wish. Thus dreams of being naked are dreams of exhibiting. (Freud, 1900a, p. 245, my emphasis)

" 'Civilized' sexual morality and modern nervous illness" (Freud, 1908d)

Kulturarbeit figures five times in " 'Civilized' sexual morality and modern nervous illness" (Freud, 1908d), which explains the significance of this work for the exploration of this notion. Let us, therefore, take a look at this text, so rich in diverse respects.

As a preliminary, Freud comments upon Christian von Ehrenfels's book *Sexualethik* (1907), in which he distinguishes between two types of morality, "natural sexual morality ... under whose dominance a human stock is able to remain in lasting possession of health and efficiency" and civilised sexual morality "obedience to which ... spurs men on to *intense and productive cultural activity*" (my emphasis). And Freud adds, "This contrast, he thinks, is best illustrated by comparing the innate character of a people with their cultural attainments" (Freud, 1908d, p. 181).

So here we have two types of morality, the second of which "spurs" all individuals to engage in *cultural activity*, which is not only intense, but also *productive*. What does he mean by cultural activity and by productive? It would probably be a matter of psychical work realised by every individual in the service of his or her society and culture, therefore having social and cultural purposes and "producing" results, both individual and collective, thus allowing each person to become an active member of society and a "participant in its culture". But what would be the nature of this psychical work and what psychical materials would be used to accomplish it?

Freud provided us with some answers. First of all, he maintained that this "civilized" sexual morality, corresponding to a third stage of civilisation "in which only legitimate reproduction is allowed as a sexual aim", and which dominated the bourgeois social order of his time, has damaging effects on individuals through the harmful suppression of their sexual lives, and in this way is conducive to "modern nervousness", that is to say neuroses and psychoneuroses. Consequently, he noted the correlation between "increasing nervous illness" and "modern civilized life", as well as the two factors causing suffering in "neurotics": their constitution and cultural requirements (Freud, 1908d, pp. 182, 185, 189–191).

In fact, through this "civilized" sexual morality, it is society and its requirements that impose instinctual repression upon its members as being one of the conditions of social integration and adaptation for each one of them. However, we find Freudian discourse to be much more complex and sophisticated. Indeed, when he writes,

Generally speaking, our civilization is built up on the suppression of instincts. Each individual has surrendered some of his possessions— some part of the sense of omnipotence or of the aggressive and vindictive inclinations in his personality. From these contributions has grown *civilization's common possession of material and ideal property*. (Freud, 1908d, p. 186, my emphasis)

It is definitely a matter of instinctual repression, but also of other things, namely, of a personal gift of part of one's instinctual capital, hostile impulses in particular, which would represent the contribution of every individual as a genuine participant in the constitution of "civilization's common possession of material and ideal property", meaning, in the constituents of all civilisation, which corresponds to the twofold dimension of *Kulturarbeit*, individual and collective. Before discovering the various aspects of this portion of instinctual capital "offered as a sacrifice" to society, let us inquire into the factors determining this renunciation. Among them, Freud seemed to allude to the Oedipus complex and the need to overcome it.

Moreover, let us observe that he emphatically stressed this notion and need to participate in this instinctual repression, without which, for diverse reasons, individuals stand in opposition to their society. For that matter, it is not solely a matter of repression, but also and above all, of displacement of instincts. Indeed, in what way is this portion of individual instinctual capital constituting a reservoir of considerable forces and energy placed "at the disposal of civilized activity" mobilisable and utilisable for social and cultural purposes, that is to say, for accomplishing *Kulturarbeit*? Through the displaceability of the sexual instinct from its original sexual aims to aims that are non-sexual, socio-cultural, but "psychically related to the first aim". Freud called this capacity to exchange instinctual aims, capacity for sublimation in which lies the sexual instinct's "value for civilization". However, he warned us about individual variations of "the original strength of the instinct" and a person's ability to sublimate it, determined by diverse constitutional and external factors, "the effects of experience and the intellectual influences upon his mental apparatus", as well as about their necessary limits. Then, he explains that the instinctual components involved in this work of sublimation are "what are known as the *perverse* elements of sexual excitation", because "unserviceable for the reproductive function". Nevertheless, they are also to some extent, suppressed (Freud, 1908d, pp. 187–189).

So it is that, according to Freud, the "forces that can be employed for *cultural activities* are thus to a great extent obtained through the suppression of what are known as the *perverse* elements of sexual excitation" (Freud, 1908d, p. 189, my emphasis) and, I might add, through their displacement through sublimation. A minority of individuals succeed in this undertaking. Others are damaged by it in various different ways.

Also following from all this is Freud's belief that *normal sexuality would cause civilisation to progress,* unlike its perverse deviations that, through the inability to mobilise sexual components in the service of *cultural activity* or *Kulturarbeit,* would be at odds with this.

But this "civilized" sexual morality also represents a form of social injustice, in that civilisation requires that all those participating in it live their sexual lives in a single way, a stricture that some accept and others reject. More than an injustice, by imposing a standardisation of human conduct, it is a matter of one of the forms of social violence.

So what about the men and women who suffer from this "civilized" sexual morality corresponding to the third stage of civilisation that requires abstinence of them? One should, moreover, distinguish between abstaining from all sexual activity in general and abstaining from sexual behaviour with the opposite sex. What kinds of harm, and what forms of compensation offered by society, did Freud observe and inventory?

First of all, he considered that the "pronounced forms of the perversions and of homosexuality . . . make those subject to them socially useless and unhappy" and that "in order to effect this suppression of their sexual instinct, they use up the forces which they would otherwise employ in *cultural activities.* They are, as it were, inwardly inhibited and outwardly paralysed" (Freud, 1908d, p. 190, my emphasis).

Then, once again, he envisaged nervous illness as another form of harm, both personal and to society. At this point, I shall stop my discussion of this remarkable sociological text, which is also of socio-historical value.

"Thoughts for the times on war and death" (Freud, 1915b)

This text seems to me to be just as remarkable as the foregoing one in several diverse respects. Apart from the appearance of a new occurrence of *work of civilization* or *Kulturarbeit*—in its collective dimension here—the presentation of some ideas about the individual and collective morality of peoples and nations, about war and death, with the notion of *cultural and conventional attitude* of civilised human beings (Freud, 1915b, p. 290), Freud also presents the principal characteristics of *Kulturarbeit*, its conditions, processes, and purposes, and a completely new notion of *cultural hypocrisy* (Freud, 1915b, p. 284) upon which all civilisation is also based. Nevertheless, we already sensed this in *The Interpretation of Dreams* with the need to distort and disguise latent dream thoughts under the pressure of mental censorship analogous to social constraints.

To begin with, I would like to cite the text in which the collective dimension of the notion of *work of civilisation* figures. There, Freud wrote,

> Observation showed, to be sure, that embedded in these civilized states there were remnants of certain other peoples, which were universally unpopular, and had therefore been only reluctantly, and even if not fully, admitted to participation in the common work of civilization, for which they had shown themselves suitable enough. (Freud, 1915b, p. 276)

This *common work of civilisation* corresponds to social, economic, political, technological, and cultural activities in which the members of every society participate for purposes of organisation, production, preservation, reproduction, and transmission. It is a matter of "labour in society" as defined by Durkheim (Durkheim, 1893). And these "remnants of certain other peoples" share in it, though they are also objects of hostile impulses coming from the dominant majority.

Let us now turn to individual *Kulturarbeit*, its processes and aims as envisaged by Freud, who wondered, "How, in point of fact, do we imagine the process by which an individual rises to a comparatively high plane of morality?" (Freud, 1915b, p. 281).

Well, for him, it was a matter of a process of "transformation of 'bad' instincts", essentially selfish and cruel ones, brought about by two factors, internal and external, working in the same direction (Freud, 1915b, p. 282) and conditioning, or determining, the emergence of *cultural hypocrisy* on both the individual and the collective plane, something I shall return to at a later point. Prior to that, Freud had reminded readers that "the deepest essence of human nature" consists of elementary instinctual impulses that are neither good nor bad in themselves, that are similar in all people, and aim at satisfaction. On the basis of what criteria then are instincts to be called good or bad? Freud answered that we "classify them and their expressions in that way according to their relation to the needs and demands of the human community" (Freud, 1915b, p. 281).

This raises questions for us about their universality and, of course, suggests to us the existence of historical, social, and cultural differences, therefore, of unique cases and collective identities based upon this type of relation between human instinctual capital and the needs and demands of every society. The notions of modes, of means of utilisation and instinctual tolerance deserve to be inquired into here.

What, then, is the *psychosocial* fate of these impulses said to be bad? According to Freud,

> These primitive impulses undergo a lengthy process of development before they are allowed to become active in the adult. They are inhibited, directed towards other aims and fields, become commingled, alter their objects, and are to some extent turned back upon their possessor. Reaction-formations against certain instincts take the deceptive form of a change in their content, as though egoism had changed into altruism, or cruelty into pity. These reaction-formations are facilitated by the circumstance that some instinctual impulses make their appearance almost from the first in pairs of opposites . . . . (Freud, 1915b, p. 281)

This is the case of the love–hate pair combined in one and the same person and in one and the same object. And Freud concluded that, "It is not until all these 'instinctual vicissitudes' have been surmounted that what we call a person's character is formed . . . ." (Freud, 1915b, p. 282)

What are these factors at work?

The internal factor consists in the influence exercised on selfish instincts, for example, by erotic components, the adding of which transforms them into social instincts. It is a matter of an inborn disposition as "inherited organization", therefore, of one of the components of the archaic heritage of every individual—proving, then, subject to the influence of the cultural history of his or her ancestors—who successfully completes this transformation in response to environmental incentives (Freud, 1915b, pp. 282–283).

The external factor consists in the force exercised by upbringing, which is continued by the direct pressure of the socio-cultural environment. In the course of every individual's life, internal compulsion constantly replaces external compulsion, and this external factor constantly favours the transformation of selfish instincts into social instincts. Freud called this human capacity to transform selfish instincts into social instincts under the influence of erotism, "*susceptibility to culture*", which is therefore composed of an inborn part and another part acquired during one's life. The relations of these two parts to one another and to the untransformed part of instinctual life vary considerably (Freud, 1915b, pp. 282–283).

Upbringing and environment work not only with the benefits of love, but also with rewards and punishments. Based on this, Freud introduced the entirely new notion of the *cultural hypocrisy*, clearly favoured by these external factors. Indeed, under their influence, *we can act well, in the cultural sense* without this replacement of selfish instincts by social instincts having taken place in us. However, the outcome would manifestly be the same, and it would only be in particular circumstances that certain people always conduct themselves well because their instinctual dispositions compel them to do so, and that others are only good for as long as, and insofar as, their cultural behaviour brings them selfish advantages. Freud considered that civilisation not only favours the production of this hypocrisy to a great degree, but that it is also necessarily built upon it, just as it is one of the factors of the maintenance of that civilisation, because the human susceptibility to culture is not in and of itself sufficient for the realisation of that collective aim. "Thus", he found, "there are very many more cultural hypocrites than truly civilized men" (Freud, 1915b, p. 284).

The Future of an Illusion (Freud, 1927c)

Kulturarbeit, translated by *work of civilisation*, occurs four times in this text.

In every case, the term seems to refer to the collective dimension of this work consisting, on the one hand, in controlling nature in order to protect oneself from its dangers and to procure the necessities of life and, on the other hand, in establishing measures, regulations, and institutions enabling one to maintain social life, which as it happens corresponds to the tasks that Freud assigned to culture.

Before discussing the "store of religious ideas" that are part of the "psychical assets" and "psychical inventory" of a culture, Freud offers us his most complete definition of culture and indicates its principal tasks:

- Controlling the forces of nature to protect oneself and obtaining the necessities of life. He wrote of how, "With these forces nature rises up against us, majestic, cruel and inexorable; she brings to our mind once more our weaknesses and our helplessness, which we thought to escape through the *work of civilization*" (my emphasis). The "great common task" of humanity, he maintained, is that of defending itself "against the crushingly superior force of nature" (Freud, 1927c, pp. 16, 21).
- But also regulating social relationships among the members of society.

Let us remember that, for Freud, "every civilization rests on a compulsion to work" (Freud, 1927c, p. 10), both individual and collective—to be understood in the Durkheimian sense of "labour in society", presupposing a division of labour between the sexes and across generations—as well as on instinctual renunciation, which engenders considerable psychical sacrifice on the part of those participating in it, causing them to take a virtually hostile attitude to the civilisation and its multiple demands. This is the meaning of the first occurrence of *Kulturarbeit* in *The Future of an Illusion*, where Freud wrote that it "is just as impossible to do without control of the mass by a minority as it is to dispense with *coercion in the work of civilization*" (Freud, 1927c, p. 7, my emphasis). A little further on, we again encounter the same idea when Freud writes that "coercion cannot be dispensed with in the *work of civilization*" (Freud, 1927c, p. 8, my emphasis). This is why Freud declared that "every individual is virtually an enemy of civilization, though civilization is supposed to be an object of universal human interest" (Freud, 1927c, p. 6) and, consequently, must be defended against the individual. This task is effected by means of multiple regulations, prohibitions, commands, and institutions.

Indeed, the oldest human privations corresponding to universal instinctual wishes and established by prohibitions against incest, murder, and cannibalism "are still operative and still form the kernel of hostility to civilization" (Freud, 1927c, p. 10). Although those prohibitions also made possible the advent of human civilisation—freeing itself in this way from its primal animal status—the same is not true of other forms of privations, which only concern certain social categories and spare others.

However, Freud observed that present in all human beings are destructive, anti-social, and anti-cultural tendencies, themselves not reacting to the instinctual renunciation required, as well as that "a certain percentage of mankind (owing to a pathological disposition or an excess of instinctual strength) will always remain asocial" (Freud, 1927c, p. 9).

Moreover, according to Freud, the lazy and virtually dangerous nature of the human masses is "supposed to prove that coercion cannot be dispensed with in the *work of civilization*" (Freud, 1927c, p. 8, my emphasis). He argued, in addition, for the need for a minority to keep them under control, as he had already stated in 1915 in "Thoughts for the times on war and death". In *The Future of an Illusion*, he wrote, "It is just as impossible to do without control of the mass by a minority as it is to dispense with coercion in the work of civilization" (Freud, 1927c, p. 7).

The material necessities of life, the means of obtaining them and the arrangements made for their distribution do not therefore constitute the essence of culture. Alongside them are other means and "mental" assets, which can serve to safeguard it by lessening the burden of the necessary instinctual sacrifices required of people, but also by reconciling them with it through the various forms of compensation it proposes in this way. Among them, Freud cites: "the extent to which a civilization's precepts have been internalized" or "the moral level of its participants"—that is to say the intrapsychical, individual establishment of the superego; the ideals and artistic creations—that is to say, the "satisfactions that can be derived from those sources"; then the "store of religious ideas" (Freud, 1927c, pp. 12, 42).

The latter having already been abundantly explored, I shall simply cite the passage that contains the fourth occurrence of *Kulturarbeit* or *work of civilisation*. Freud's imaginary interlocutor-adversary, in fact, maintains that civilisation is built up upon religious teachings and the preservation of human society presupposes that its members believe they are true. Freud wrote,

> If men are taught that there is no almighty and all-just God, no divine world-order and no future life, they will feel exempt from all obligation to obey the precepts of civilization. Everyone will, without inhibition or

fear, follow his asocial, egoistic instincts, and seek to exercise his power. Chaos which we have banished through many thousands of years of the *work of civilization*, will come again. (Freud, 1927c, p. 34, my emphasis)

Civilization and Its Discontents (Freud, 1930a)

Let us take a look at the two occurrences of the term here.

Freud depicts for us the *sexual differentiation of men and women in terms of their relationship to civilisation*, to the *work of civilisation*, and to sublimation. While in the beginning, women had "laid the foundations of civilization by the claims of their love", they later came into opposition with its development, exercising then "a retarding and restraining influence" because they represent "the interests of family and of sexual life". And the *"work of civilization* has become increasingly the business of men. It confronts them with ever more difficult tasks and compels them to carry out instinctual sublimations of which women are little capable" (Freud, 1930a, p. 103, my emphasis), something that can only be accomplished to the detriment of men's interest in women and sexual life, consequently estranging them from their roles as husbands and fathers. So, driven into the background by the "claims of civilization", women will develop a hostile attitude toward civilisation. Moreover, the constraints imposed by economic necessity oblige civilisation to withdraw from sexuality out of its own need to consume a great amount of psychical energy, and Freud observed that our western European civilisation dominated by a bourgeois social order has reached a "high-water mark in such a development" (Freud, 1930a, p. 104).

I find there some basic conflicts underscored by Freud:

- Between women as representatives of the interests of the family, and of sexual life, and culture.
- Between men and women in their relationship to culture and to the *work of civilisation*.
- Between the *work of civilisation* and sexuality through the mediation of the necessary work of instinctual sublimation, which impoverishes the erotic instinctual capital, and its dangers of instinctual defusion.
- Between aim-inhibited and sublimated homosexual bonds prevailing within the male work community and the heterosexuality of conjugal bonds.

- Between sexuality, as autonomous source of pleasure, and marriage, as procreative bond between a man and a woman. Society would impose upon all its members a single kind of genital sexual life based on a choice of a single heterosexual object—therefore ruling out multiplicity of choices, the homosexual object, and perversions.

But culture does not settle for withdrawing from sexuality the energy necessary to accomplish the *work of civilisation*—therefore, necessary to the inevitable instinctual sublimations—or for promoting "bonds of common work and common interests", or requiring a single, therefore, quite restrictive heterosexual sexuality. It also seeks to establish other kinds of ties, libidinal in nature, among its participants by means of identifications and aim-inhibition for purposes of strengthening communal bonds (Freud, 1930a, pp. 108–109).

Freud asked what the main reason for this would be.

He answered that the primal, autonomous instinct of aggression and destruction of human beings, offshoot and representative of the death instinct, is at the origin of the primary hostility of human beings towards one another and actually threatens all of society with disintegration, and he said that culture, in fact, encounters its most potent obstacle in it—to be distinguished from the human hostility towards civilisation inherent in the instinctual renunciation dominating social relations, and against which culture must protect itself.

This is why, if culture or cultural development is a process in the service of Eros, but also the work of Eros—which unfolds on the scale of humanity and aspires to combine single individuals, then communities libidinally bound to one another into one great unity constituting humanity—the human instinct of aggression manifests its opposition to this "programme of civilization". Consequently, according to Freud, this development of culture shows us the struggle between Eros and death, the instinct of life and the instinct of destruction as it works itself out on the level of the human species. As Freud explained, "This struggle is what all life essentially consists of, and the evolution of civilization may therefore be simply described as the struggle for life of the human species" (Freud, 1930a, p. 122).

So, what are the means that culture has at its disposal that require a considerable expenditure of energy, in order to inhibit, neutralise, this major danger to society, perhaps deactivate this aggressive instinct?

In addition to the identifications and aim-inhibited love relation-ships already mentioned, Freud detected reaction-formations and the ideal commandment "to love thy neighbour as thyself", in particular. That is not all. This aggressive instinct can find a means of satisfac-tion in hostile behaviour toward those outside the social community, especially those belonging to adjoining communities, which makes it possible to strengthen the cohesion of the former. Freud wrote,

> I gave this phenomenon the name of "the narcissism of minor differ-ences", a name which does not do much to explain it. We can now see that it is a convenient and relatively harmless satisfaction of the incli-nation to aggression, by means of which cohesion between members of the community is made easier. (Freud, 1930a, p. 114)

Let us now look at the method deemed the most determinant and significant that Freud studied concerning the course of individual development. Once again it is a matter of an analogy between the individual and collective domains. It is a matter of the establishment of the superego or conscience in each individual and the correlative advent of the sense of guilt, expression of tension between the ego and the superego. Culture, work of Eros and in its service, interacts with the increase of this sense of guilt and can only realise its aims by those means. Nevertheless, this also represents the most important problem of cultural development inasmuch as it constitutes the price to be paid for this progress finding expression in an inevitable loss of happiness.

From this perspective, but on the collective plane, let us look at the hypothetical production of the superego by society as a whole, or the *cultural superego*, comparable to the individual superego, under whose influence cultural development would be effected. It produces its ideals and makes its demands, disobedience of which is punished by "fear of conscience". Among those demands, ethics brings together those con-cerning the relations of human beings to one another, or social relations, and Freud conceives of it as a "therapeutic attempt—in an endeavour to achieve, by means of a command of the super-ego, something which has so far not been achieved by means of any other cultural activities" (Freud, 1930a, p. 142). The second occurrence of *Kulturarbeit* therefore makes its appearance here, translated this time by *cultural activities*. Other phenomena of cultural development could then be made intelli-gible through the influence of this cultural superego.

"Lecture XXXI: The dissection of the psychical personality" in
New Introductory Lectures on Psycho-analysis (Freud, 1933a)

The final occurrence of *Kulturarbeit* in Freud's work appears at the end
of this lecture, where it has been translated by *work of culture* and
refers to the essential aim of all individual psychoanalytical work and,
through that, of all psychical work having to be accomplished by all
individuals. Indeed, Freud tells us that all psychical work is *work of
culture*, but, after the fashion of the draining of the Zuider Zee, it takes
place on such a great scale that it is endlessly being unveiled. The
intention of psychoanalysis, he explained,

> is, indeed, to strengthen the ego, to make it more independent of the
> super-ego, to widen its field of perception and enlarge its organiza-
> tion, so that it can appropriate fresh portions of the id. Where the id
> was, there ego shall be. It is a *work of culture*—not unlike the draining
> of the Zuider Zee. (Freud, 1933a, Lecture XXXI, p. 80)

This "ego" task of domination and mastery of the id through the
conquest and appropriation of "new fragments" of this "primal
animal status" of human nature are to me suggestive of a recurrent
Freudian analogy, that of the domination of the forces of nature,
which still falls within the scope of that nineteenth century bourgeois
ideology instituting the triumph of reason and progress. These two
essential tasks of the *domination of nature* in its different forms consequently come under *Kulturarbeit*.

Necessary exploration of other texts

"Formulations on the two principles of mental functioning"
(Freud, 1911b)

This text, which falls within the theoretical framework of the first
topic and the first theory of instincts, makes it possible to study individual *Kulturarbeit* with respect to its task of constituting a differentiated psychical apparatus adapted to the demands of the external
world, of reality, as well as being active with regard to it and capable
of modifying it. It also demystifies the role the external world plays in
this psychical work and the "psychological significance" it correlatively assumes (Freud, 1911b, p. 218).

Thus, replacement of the pleasure principle by the reality principle, which Freud considered to be a "revolution in the mind", in this way leads to the transformation of a pleasure-ego into a reality-ego that strives for what is useful and guards itself against damage. It sums up the principal task of education (Freud, 1911b, pp. 223–224).

Totem and Taboo (Freud, 1912–1913)

Although the word *Kulturarbeit* never appears in this work, its presence is often implied, especially as concerns the phylogenesis of culture. So, I shall present some reflections and notions particularly useful for my construction of this notion.

In the second chapter of the book, "Taboo and emotional ambivalence", Freud once again expressed his conviction regarding the methodological importance of the psychology of neuroses for understanding socio-cultural formations and the development of culture, something that enabled him to extend his exploration of similarities between other forms of neuroses and cultural formations, as well as to inquire into the essential instinctual differences between those two types of formations. If taboos and obsessional neuroses share the basic ambivalence of emotions, they differ in that taboos are social formations, cultural creations, while neuroses are individual, asocial formations, which "endeavour to achieve by private means what is effected in society by collective effort" (Freud, 1912–1913, p. 73). Instinctual sexual forces, in fact, exercise a major influence there on social instincts, while cultural formations are based upon social instincts coming from combining egotistic and erotic elements. Thus, Freud would have us observe that,

> The neuroses exhibit on the one hand striking and far-reaching points of agreement with those great social institutions, art, religion and philosophy. But on the other hand they seem like distortions of them. It might be maintained that a case of hysteria is a caricature of a work of art, that an obsessional neurosis is a caricature of a religion and that a paranoic delusion is a caricature of a philosophical system. (Freud, 1912–1913, p. 73)

Highlighting the omnipotence of thoughts in primitive people as evidence in favour of narcissism and as governing magic, Freud therefore proposed a new comparison between the stages of development of mankind's view of the universe as borrowed from the British evolutionist anthropologists (Tylor and Frazer) and the stages of the individual's libidinal development:

> The animistic phase would correspond to narcissism both chronologically and in its content; the religious phase would correspond to the stage of object-choice of which the characteristic is a child's attachment to his parents; while the scientific phase would have an exact counterpart in the stage at which an individual has reached maturity, has renounced the pleasure principle, adjusted himself to reality and turned to the external world for the object of his desires. (Freud, 1912–1913, p. 90)

I would now like to take some ideas essential for my exploration of the notion of *Kulturarbeit* from the chapter entitled "The return of totemism in childhood".

Freud first recounts for us the myth of the creation of culture or phylogenesis of human culture—which, by the way, blends in with the phylogenesis of *Kulturarbeit*—inaugurated by the collective killing of the father of the primal horde by the company of the sons. The creation of human culture is consequently correlative to a collective crime that produced a creative, atoning consciousness of guilt in the authors of the crime, the company of the brothers. We are presented with reflections on the very beginnings of religion, morality, law, as well as on the nature of social bonds. In addition, on the basis of the notion of "ineradicable traces" (Freud, 1912–1913, p. 155) passed down to subsequent generations by this criminal deed and the resulting collective consciousness of guilt, Freud examines and introduces the necessary hypothesis of the existence of a *collective mind*, without which, according to him, a psychology of peoples would be inconceivable (Freud, 1912–1913, pp. 157–158). And I might add, without which any culture in itself is inconceivable, because I consider the *collective mind* to be one of the fundamental components of all culture. Freud actually considered totemism to be both an institution and representative of the first phase of human culture, the understanding of which should be both historical and psychological, thus informing us about the conditions of its emergence and development, as well as the human psychical needs it symbolises.

Freud's methodological approach led him *in fine* to establish the Oedipus complex as a link between the two fields—intrapsychical-individual and collective, social, and cultural—on the basis of a certain number of needs, capacities, and processes of human mental activity, but also taking into consideration an essential analogy between individuals and society, that of a mind—in the one case individual, in the other a collective—within which we inevitably find similar processes. Among these, I shall mention phantasy, symbolisation, sublimation, and projection, the last one as a shaping of the external world based on internal perceptions. Psyche and culture are correlative, therefore interrelated. He concludes,

> At the conclusion, then, of this exceedingly condensed inquiry, I should like to insist that its outcome shows that the beginnings of religion, morality, and society and art converge in the Oedipus complex. This is in complete agreement with the psycho-analytic finding that the same complex constitutes the nucleus of all neuroses, so far as our present knowledge goes. It seems to me a most surprising discovery that the problems of social psychology, too, should prove soluble on the basis of one single concrete point—man's relation to his father. It is even possible that yet another psychological problem belongs in this same connection. I have often had occasion to point out that emotional ambivalence in the proper sense of the term—that is, the simultaneous existence of love and hate towards the same object—lies at the root of many important cultural institutions. We know nothing of the origin of this ambivalence. (Freud, 1912–1913, pp. 156–157)

But that collective criminal deed founding culture—totemic during the first phase of its development—Freud speculated, inevitably had to leave ineradicable traces in the history of humanity and finds expression in substitutes, whose purpose is to disguise and expunge all memory, something that led him to consider the necessary hypothesis of a *collective mind*. Indeed, this hypothesis—which Freud takes as a basic principle and in which psychical processes are carried out *as in the psychical life of an individual*—is the basis of the existence of the psychology of people, ensures continuity in people's emotional life over generations, especially as concerns the consciousness of guilt resulting from the brothers' collective criminal deed, which would persist in generations of people knowing nothing about it, but also conditions all progress and all development, both individual and collective, something that is to be associated with the Freudian theory that culture rests on repressions effected by earlier generations and that each new generation is required to effect these same forms of repression in order to maintain that culture.

Freud pursues his inquiry asking, "how much can we attribute to psychical continuity in the sequence of generations? and what are the ways and means employed by one generation in order to hand on its mental states to the next one?" (Freud, 1912–1913, p. 158).

Apart from the means of direct communication and of the tradition mentioned, Freud held that part of the task would be ensured by what he called the *inheritance of psychical dispositions*, "which, however, need to be given some impetus in the life of the individual before they can be roused into actual operation. This may be the meaning of the poet's words . . . 'What thou hast inherited from thy fathers, acquire it to make it thine' " (Freud, 1912–1913, p. 158 and note).

In addition, he maintained that no mental impulse suppressed in one generation would be exempt from traces in the subsequent generations, no matter what forms they take. In other words, no generation would be able to hide from the following processes and psychical contents of whatever significance, which must then make room for surrogate—therefore distorted—impulses and for reactions resulting from them, something that correlates with the capacity all human beings have by virtue of their unconscious mental activity to interpret the reactions of other human beings, meaning, to undo again the distortions to which the other person has resorted in expressing his or her emotional impulses (Freud, 1912–1913, p. 159).

René Kaës (1993) considers that, above and beyond his phylogenetic thesis, Freud proposed to us the notion of *work of psychical transmission across generations and over generations*, defined and understood as the process and result of psychical relationships between psychical apparatuses and as transformations effected by these relationships. It allows for the notion—verifiable in formations of tombs and ghosts—of a non-work of psychical transmission. It requires differentiation between what is transmitted and what is received and transformed, particularly in the process of historicisation of the subject, that is to say, in the process of appropriation of the subject of the heritage and of the transmission by the I, which assumes the thought of it and situates it. It makes "afterwardness" the main category of the thought of the origin of the psychical process and of what is to come. It projects the phylogenetic hypothesis into its fruitful heuristic space, that of interpretative reinsertion, and not that of linear causality (Kaës, 1993, p. 58).

Group Psychology and the Analysis of the Ego (Freud, 1921c)

In this work, Freud explored some characteristic aspects of a "group", and especially its "soul", its processes, and its formations. He also raised questions about the relationships between *Kulturarbeit* and the conditions for any individual to be a member of a "group", as well as the intrapsychical effects of this.

Moses and Monotheism (Freud, 1939a)

In *Moses and Monotheism* (Freud, 1939a), Freud proposed several themes for our reflection, certain of which are presented and developed in the section devoted to religion as an institution, but also that on the notion of archaic heritage, which I plan to explore. Then, I shall turn to the *fabrication of the identity of a people* by a "great man" inspired by a "great idea", religion, an example of the collective field of *Kulturarbeit* and of the twofold role played by religion in identity structuring, both individual and collective.

The notion of archaic heritage

I have not found any mention of this notion of archaic heritage anywhere prior to its first occurrence in "Instincts and their vicissitudes" (Freud, 1915c).

Beginning in 1915, and up until the years 1938–1939, with *Moses and Monotheism* and "An outline of psycho-analysis" (Freud, 1940a), Freud endeavoured to define, circumscribe, locate in the mind, and give a content to this archaic heritage, with which the synonyms of phylogenetic heritage, the individual's phylogenetic acquisition, and archaic inheritance are associated.

According to him, this archaic "animal heritage . . . comprises all the forces that are required for the subsequent cultural development of the individual, but they must first be sorted out and worked over". And he explained that "the overcoming of the Oedipus complex coincides with the most efficient way of mastering the archaic, animal heritage of humanity" (Freud, 1919g, p. 262).

In *Moses and Monotheism*, he reminded readers that at work in the psychical life of individuals are not only *what they have experienced themselves*, but also what was *innately present in them at birth*, elements of phylogenetic origin, an *archaic heritage*.

Memory traces tied to something experienced by earlier generations persist in the mental lives of individuals as elements with a
phylogenetic origin and constitute their archaic heritage (Freud,
1939a, pp. 98–99).

He then asked "what this consists in, what it contains, and what is
the evidence for it" and proposed this answer,

> The immediate and most certain answer is that it consists in certain
> [innate] dispositions such as are characteristic of all living organisms:
> in the capacity and tendency, that is, to enter particular lines of devel-
> opment and to react in a particular manner to certain excitations,
> impressions and stimuli. Since experience shows that there are distinc-
> tions in this respect between individuals of the human species, the
> archaic heritage must include these distinctions; they represent what
> we recognize as the *constitutional* factor in the individual. (Freud,
> 1939a, p. 98)

He first of all cites "the universality of symbolism in language, . . .
original knowledge" (Freud, 1939a, p. 98) detectable in children and
in the dreams of adults, emanating from the time of the development
of speech and suggesting the existence of "the inheritance of an intellectual disposition" occurring again during the development of
speech. He then turns to the reactions to early traumas, which would
be evidence of an inheritance of "subject-matter" (Freud, 1939a, p. 99),
in particular, of memory traces of experiences of earlier generations
inferred from "the residual phenomena of the work of analysis",
something giving people a new way, according to Freud, to bridge
"the gulf between individual and group psychology" and "deal with
peoples as we do with an individual neurotic" (Freud, 1939a, p. 100)—
audacity in which Freud allowed himself to indulge. Thus,

> The behaviour of neurotic children towards their parents in the
> Œdipus and castration complex abounds in such reactions, which
> seem unjustified in the individual case and only become intelligible
> phylogenetically—by their connection with the experience of earlier
> generations. (Freud, 1939a, p. 99)

But the principal memory trace is that of the killing of the primal
father, which would enter the archaic heritage of the "*human animal*",
corresponding to "the instincts of animals even though it is different
in its compass and contents" (Freud, 1939a, p. 100), under certain

conditions, whenever the event was sufficiently important, or re-peated often enough, or both. Moreover, this repressed memory can become active during the awakening of its trace "by a real recent repetition of the event". So it was with the murder of Moses and later that of Christ (Freud, 1939a, p. 101).

This notion of archaic heritage therefore seems to have been for Freud *what establishes the connection between phylogenesis and ontogenesis*, as well as between individual and collective psychologies.

What are the contents according to Freud?

- The extensive *instinctual ambivalence* in "Instincts and their vicissitudes" (Freud, 1915c).
- The *primal phantasies*, which belong to the archaic heritage as "disposition to reacquisition".
- The *affects*, residues of recollections of prehistoric times.
- The *"enigmatic phobias"*, among them, fear of being alone, of the dark, of strangers, as reactions to the danger of object loss.
- Both the *development of the ego and of the libido*, which would also be "heritages, abbreviated recapitulations of the development which all mankind has passed through from its primaeval days over long periods of time . . . what is at bottom inherited is nevertheless freshly acquired in the development of the individual". And Freud added that "the power which forced a development of this kind upon humanity and maintains its pressure in the same direction to-day . . . is, once again, frustration by reality . . . the pressure of vital needs—Necessity ('Aνάγχη [Ananke]) . . . a strict educator" (Freud, 1916–1917, pp. 345–355).
- *The symbolic relation*, never learned by the individual, is also to be considered as a phylogenetic heritage.

What evidence is there for these claims?

Dreams and neuroses would be "preservers" of the contents of archaic heritage, as well as cultural products, like the most ancient legends and ancient customs, among other things.

The making of the identity of the Jewish people

"How is it possible for a single man to evolve such extraordinary effectiveness that he can form a people out of random individuals and families, can stamp them with their definitive character and determine their fate for thousands of years?" (Freud, 1939a, p. 107), Freud wondered.

He considered that great persons influence their contemporaries in two ways, through their personalities and through the idea to which they commit themselves, which "may stress some *ancient wishful image of the masses* (my emphasis) or it may point out a new wishful aim, or it may cast its spell over them in some other way". Sometimes—and Freud considered this to be certainly the more primary of the two— the personality, with obvious paternal characteristics, acts alone and the idea plays very minimal role (Freud, 1939a, p. 109).

And Moses did indeed represent a paternal model for the Jews. He made them "his dear children", and it became difficult for them to distinguish his image from that of his god (Freud, 1939a, p. 110). The specific particularities of Moses' religion therefore acted upon the Jewish people and left a lasting imprint on their character.

The particularly high opinion they have of themselves, considering themselves superior to others from whom they have kept apart by many of their customs, and their self-confidence, are character traits conferred by Moses and derived from the belief that they are the chosen people of God, whose Exodus from Egypt, later commemorated by the feast of Passover, in particular served as proof. A "religious anchorage" resulted from that, and from then on that feeling became part of their religious belief. "Owing to their especially intimate relation to their God, they acquired a share in his grandeur" (Freud, 1939a, p. 106).

The prohibition against making an image of God had a profound effect. It was a question of a new abstract, intellectual way of representing God. It thus meant pushing sensory perception into the background in favour of an abstraction, a victory of intellectuality over sensuality. And God was raised to a higher degree of intellectuality. The result of all the progress of this nature was to intensify people's feelings of self-esteem, to make them proud, so that they felt superior to others who had remained "under the spell of sensuality". These advances in intellectuality opened for them the way to sublimations, and especially to holding intellectual work in high esteem. Finally, the importance accorded to ethics, its commands and prohibitions, leading to many an instinctual renunciation, derived its origin in the consciousness of guilt due to the repression of hostility towards God, a component of the ambivalent relationship.

Moses sanctified his people through circumcision, a symbolic substitute for castration, therefore, a sign of submission to God's will, keeping them apart from others. Their cohesiveness consisted in an ideal factor, the common possession of a certain intellectual and emotional wealth, whence the absence of troubles linked to mixtures of blood. And their hard fates and genuine disillusionment have reinforced these tendencies.

But, Freud observed that it "is not obvious and not immediately understandable why an advance in intellectuality, a set-back to sensuality should raise the self-regard both of an individual and of a people" (Freud, 1939a, p. 116). He replied that, "Perhaps men simply pronounce that what is more difficult is higher, and their pride is merely their narcissism augmented by the consciousness of a difficulty overcome" (Freud, 1939a, p. 118).

And the great man Moses was precisely the authority for the love of whom the Jewish people accomplished this evolution, and since he himself owed his effectiveness to his resemblance to the father, the role of superego of this people fell to him.

My construction of the notion of Kulturarbeit

Phylogenetic aspects of Kulturarbeit

From a *phylogenetic* point of view, according to Freud, the first stage and manifestation of *Kulturarbeit* was that accomplished by human beings in order to create *culture* with its institutions, its basic rules, its customs and ritual practices, its beliefs, and its systems of representations, the first product of a hypothetical "collective mind", as he termed it.

Theoretical speculations led Freud to *imagine* that it was *organic repression* that opened the way to culture and, in particular, triumphed over anal eroticism. According to him, the cultural process was inaugurated by the upright posture of human beings, which led to a whole set of correlative phenomena, such as a denigration of the olfactory stimuli to which anal eroticism would succumb and would determine the cultural aspiration to cleanliness, the prevailance of visual stimuli, the acquisition of visibility of genital organs covered up until then and from then on requiring protection, an arousal of feelings of shame, isolation during the menstrual period, continuity of sexual excitation, up to the founding of the primitive family, and through that up to the threshold of human culture.

According to Freud, the collective murder of the father of the primal horde, followed by his being devoured by the company of sons set this in motion. Feeling profound emotional ambivalence towards their father, at once loved, admired, feared, and hated, the latter satisfied their hostility by the criminal deed and their desire to identify themselves with him by the cannibalistic act. Then their tenderness expressed itself in the form of collective repentance and a sense of guilt on each one's part, which then incited them to reinstate the father figure through the creation of a substitute, of a *symbol*, Durkheim would say, the totem, but also to establish basic prohibitions, those of totemism, consistent then with the two repressed desires of the Oedipus complex and also determined by the need to preserve the cohesiveness of the clan of the brothers based in particular on sublimated homosexual bonds. For Freud, these prohibitions, therefore, reflected the most ancient prohibitions created by human society: the prohibition of incest, the prohibition of murder, and the prohibition of cannibalism.

Among these first primal institutions, Freud cited religion, morality, law, and the beginnings of a social order or an initial form of social organisation, which are interdependent.

In his "Short account of psycho-analysis", he explained that they have as their "fundamental aim the enabling of the individual to master his Oedipus complex and to divert his libido from its infantile attachments into the social ones that are ultimately desired" (Freud, 1924f, p. 208).

Religion, totemic at first, originating in the sons' "consciousness of creative guilt", arising out of their own ambivalent conflict, represents both a "contract with the father", but also an attempt to appease this feeling and to propitiate the offended father through obedience after the fact. However, the ritual totemic meal also commemorated the memory of the victory over this primitive father, and the collective ingestion of his substance by the brothers reinforced their social feelings.

Morality is "restriction of instincts", therefore a limiting of the members of the totemic clan's opportunities for satisfaction. It begins with, and is based on, the basic taboo prohibitions, while *the first law* corresponds to these first taboo dictates. It represents the "power of the community", which opposes and replaces the "power of the individual", that of the father of the primal horde, condemned as "brute violence", and is conditioned and made possible by morality. Finally, this replacement of the power of the individual by that of the community represents, according to Freud, the "decisive cultural step". The subsequent cultural demand would be that of justice.

The first form of social organisation then came into existence with instinctual renunciation, recognition of reciprocal obligations, and the establishment of institutions declared "inviolable".

As for the prohibition of incest, this was to have led to exogamy and necessitated the exchanging of women among groups of men.

And, according to Freud, this human culture "rests on two pillars, one of which is the control of natural forces and the other the restriction of our instincts" (Freud, 1925e, p. 219), that is to say of the "primal animal status" of human beings, or the collective and individual aspects of *Kulturarbeit*.

Kulturarbeit was, in fact, to become work involving two poles or fields of activities, social and individual, the latter combining the two spaces, physical and psychical.

Collective Kulturarbeit

Let us first of all look at the social pole. It is a matter of *labour in society* in Durkheim's sense of the word (Durkheim, 1893), implying, therefore, social division.

On many occasions, mainly in *The Future of an Illusion* (1927c) and *Civilization and Its Discontents* (1930a), Freud discussed the needs and functions of culture, its duties and obligations towards its participants, as well as its expectations, demands, and rights with regard to them. Structured in terms of the twofold difference of sexes and generations, every society maintains a social division of the activities necessary to its good functioning and establishes systems of prohibitions, dictates, norms, and values, as well as creating numerous institutions and systems of collective representations. All that contributes to its own production, its organisation, its cohesiveness, its self-preservation, and its reproduction. It is also supposed to respond to the basic material and psychical needs of its members. From the perspective of its self-preservation and of its members need for safety, it also sets up measures for protecting against numerous dangers, in particular, those coming from its natural milieu, but above all those inherent to human hostility among its members or strangers to the community.

Culture, therefore, *works* to neutralise this aggressive human instinct, on the one hand, by continually seeking modes of social relations ensuring its cohesion. According to Freud, they would mainly consist of inhibiting the aim of sexual instincts, favouring enduring social bonds, sublimating the homosexual libido, and kindling strong feelings of identification. On the other hand, another means would be the creation of a store of cultural ideals, collective representations—religious ones in particular—but also works of art, qualified as "psychical assets", something I shall come back to. They, in fact, participate in the development of a common inheritance constituting a cultural identity and generating feelings of social belonging.

The establishment of a cultural superego, an agency belonging to the collective mind, according to Freud, comparable to the individual superego and corresponding to the latter, under the influence of which cultural development would be carried out, would produce these cultural ideals and impose its demands, the non-observance of which is punished by "fear of conscience" or "social fear". Among the latter, ethics brings together those concerning social relations. It would participate with the superego in the neutralisation of the aggressive instinct. Freud conceived of it as "a therapeutic attempt—as an endeavour to achieve, by means of a command of the super-ego, something which has so far not been achieved by means of any other cultural activities" (Freud, 1930a, p. 142).

Through the aggressive, narcissistic, libidinal renunciation required, culture imposes sacrifices on those participating in it. So, it is duty-bound to compensate them by offering them compromise solutions, a source of surrogate satisfactions. These are, Freud thought, the cultural ideals and works of art that procure its members new forms of satisfactions of a narcissistic kind. In addition, religion would be another gift of culture to those participating in it. Its "grandeur" rests on the accomplishment of three functions corresponding to the satisfaction of people's basic needs: the desire to know; relief of their anxiety in face of the life's dangers and vicissitudes, and comfort in unhappiness; and finally, precepts, prohibitions, and restrictions, by way of rules for conducting their lives. It is an attempt to control the world of the senses by means of the world of infantile wishes ever alive in every adult.

Religion would also offer a social solution to the ambivalent conflict with the father owing to its being a universal neurosis protecting all subjects from individual neurosis. In addition, it obliges prohibition of thought for the sake of its own self-preservation.

According to Freud, these religious representations are born out of the need to make human helplessness bearable, meaning that situation of human anxiety and weakness inherent in the ultra-powerful world of the forces of nature. They have an infantile model, therefore, that are built out of memories of the helplessness of the individual's own childhood and that of the human species.

Moreover, all culture *works* towards the *constitution* and *transmission* of a heritage that would include a hereditary portion, "the archaic heritage". For Freud, this notion of archaic heritage, therefore, seems to establish a link between phylogenesis and ontogenesis, the latter constituting an abbreviated recapitulation of the development of mankind. This goes back to Ernst Haeckel's biogenetic law that "ontogenesis recapitulates phylogenesis", or rather psychogenesis recapitulates sociogenesis, according to Elias (Elias, 1939). Archaic heritage would involve innate contents and specific instinctual and thought dispositions. Certain contents in its inventory become mixed up with acquired innate dispositions, as well as with primal phantasies and the developments of the ego and the libido. Let us cite, among others:

- The symbolic, "symbolic language", or "symbolic relation" consisting in thought relations between diverse objects, representations that are constituted during the historical development of language and must be repeated during the individual development of the language.
- *"Extensive" instinctual ambivalence* referring to the historical development of the coexistence between impulses with an active aim, the oldest ones, and later impulses with a passive aim, hence the notion of extensiveness of ambivalence.
- *Primal phantasies* as "disposition to re-acquisition" during individual development.
- *Affects*, residues of recollections of prehistoric times.

Culture, therefore, has a duty to transmit this heritage to its participants, securing intergenerational bonds, those with the history of humanity, but also those with the members of society sharing this "common cultural property".

But *Kulturarbeit* also consists of *cultural development* work, which operates using the same means as those of the individual, presenting analogies with the organic process and involving inevitable changes. Freud showed us that it is hindered by some forms of resistance—notably by the superego and past ideal formations—with regard to new situations.

In addition, Freud draws us a picture of male/female *sexual differentiation* with regard to culture, *Kulturarbeit,* and sublimation. While in the beginning, women "laid the foundations of civilization by the claims of their love", they later came into opposition with its development, exercising then "a retarding and restraining influence" because they represent "the interests of family and of sexual life". And, "the work of civilization has become increasingly the business of men, it confronts them with ever more difficult tasks and compels them to carry out instinctual sublimations of which women are little capable" (Freud, 1930a, p. 103), something that can only be accomplished to the detriment of their interest in women and sexual life, consequently estranging them from their roles as husbands and fathers.

Finally, every society has expectations and rights with regard to its members, as well as possessing and imposing numerous requirements upon them. Among them, Freud differentiated those that are "useful", of vital importance, from those deemed "useless", but nevertheless important, such as beauty, cleanliness, and order. The claims of justice, on the other hand, help regulate social relations, something that now brings us to the individual field of *Kulturarbeit*.

Individual Kulturarbeit

One of the aims of *Kulturarbeit*, Freud thought, is to make all subjects moral and social. So, following his thought through his numerous writings, I shall distinguish the work accomplished by every society on the body and bodily functions of its members from the psychical work realised by the ego and imposed by culture upon each one of its participants from childhood on.

The work on the body and bodily functions

The major stages of the life cycle of every individual (birth, puberty, initiation, marriage, death) will be *marked* by "rites of passage" (van

Gennep, 1909) often involving procedures performed on the body (deformations, piercings, extracting or sharpening of teeth, circumcision, excision of the clitoris, and other types of ablation, scarification, tattooing) modifying the natural state of the body, and performed in accordance with rules particular to each society. This *bodily marking* enables a collectivity as a whole, as well as each one of its members, to express the specific character of a collective and/or individual identity. Through it, a person manifests his or her status and social affiliation. Among the multiple modes of bodily marking, circumcision attracted Freud's interest, especially in *Totem and Taboo* and *Moses and Monotheism*.

Thus, in *Moses and Monotheism*, he presented circumcision as a sign of the "sanctification" of the Jewish people by Moses, their founder, a visible sign marking this people off from others, thus becoming a sign of identity, a source of narcissistic satisfaction. Moreover, as a symbolic substitute for castration, it would symbolise this people's submission to their founding father.

This work of *bodily marking* asserted itself as a form of *work of collective symbolisation* characteristic of *Kulturarbeit*.

I would also like to mention the *work undertaken with respect to certain bodily functions*, in particular with respect to every human child's excretory functions, something I call "sphincter training" or toilet-training.

Indeed, children learn to be secretive about their coprophilous tendencies and instincts connected with their excretory functions, which little by little succumb to repression. They learn to be ashamed of them and feel disgust for their objects. In two complementary texts, Freud elaborated the twofold dimension, individual and collective, of this aspect of *Kulturarbeit*.

Thus, in his *Introductory Lectures on Psycho-Analysis* (Freud, 1916–1917), Freud presented readers, in a very illuminating way, the *necessary social violence* of the process leading to a form of disappropriation of the individual's bodily functions and his or her relationship to them. However, he also envisaged possible displacements, symbolic "instinctual transpositions" institutionalised in the diverse forms of gifts to loved ones and of money, as well as "social respectability" in exchange for lost pleasure. Exchanging "pleasure for social respectability" (Freud, 1916–1917, p. 73) is actually one of the aims of education, therefore, of *Kulturarbeit*.

In the second text, drawn from *Civilization and Its Discontents*, it is a matter of the socio-cultural purpose of sphincter training, necessary individual and collective cleanliness determining respect for others, therefore, a "cultural trend towards cleanliness" (Freud, 1930a, p. 100).

Work on the psyche

As for the psychical work accomplished by the ego, Freud presented two dialectically opposed and complementary processes: the humanisation of the "human animal" through "introjection of socio-cultural components" and its socialisation or incorporation into society conferring upon it several social roles and statuses, therefore transforming the human animal from the state of "individual" into that of a "person", to use Mauss' term (Mauss, 1924), or of a "subject".

By the process of humanisation of the "human animal", I understand the pressure exercised by society and its culture, therefore, by "reality", by the "external world", in keeping with the expressions used by Freud, both upon the constitution of a differentiated psychical apparatus and the specific characteristics of its functioning and upon the obligatory instinctual transformation consecutive to renunciation. The psychogenesis of humanity, according to Freud, is characterised by an essential process of internalisation, of psychisation of phenomena and human experiences, from sensory perceptions to representations. Prohibitions, inhibitions, and external constraints would also be internalised to constitute, at a later point, "historical sediments" belonging to mankind's archaic heritage and transmissible during the ontogenesis of each person.

The constitution of a differentiated psychical apparatus and the specific characteristics of its functioning as found in Freud's writings

If one places oneself within the context of the *first topic*, the substitution of the reality principle for the pleasure principle leads to a series of adaptations of the psychical apparatus involving in particular: the institution of the activities of consciousness (attention, act of judgment, thought process . . .); the emergence and development of the preconscious system animated by the thought processes whose connection with word representations conditions access to the consciousness; repression (primal and in the strict sense) and the establishment of the first, then the second, censorship.

From the perspective of the *second topic*, according to Freud, if we must attribute the differentiation of the ego and the id not only to primitive humans, but—since it is the necessary expression of the influence of the external world—also to much simpler living beings, then, because born out of experiences that determined the establishment of totemic culture, the separation between the ego and the superego would represent the most significant traits of the development of the individual and of the species.

The sense organ of the entire apparatus, the ego dominates access to motility, but has slipped thought work in between need and action. It maintains alliances with culture and its current demands, although it is also in conflict with reality, which refers to the historical conflict between individual and society. It shares with culture the same aspiration to unity, that of Eros.

Plunging its roots into the id, and heir to the Oedipus complex, more precisely to the castration complex, through its functions of self-observation, of conscience, and of ideal, the "institution of the super-ego" constitutes one of the major accomplishments of *Kulturarbeit* realised on each individual's psyche. This creation–establishment of the superego is a "most precious cultural asset in the psychological field" (Freud, 1927c, p. 11). The people in which it is realised go from being the adversaries of culture they once were to being *vehicles of culture*, hence also the idea of "participants in the culture".

Built upon the model of the parental superego, becoming "impersonal" later on, the child's superego fills up with the same content and thus becomes "the vehicle of tradition and of all the time-resisting judgements of value which have propagated themselves in this manner from generation to generation" (Freud 1933a, Lecture XXXI, p. 67), something that also ensures psychical continuity between them. However, yielding only slowly to the influences of the present, therefore to changes, the past continues to live in the "ideologies of the super-ego". This is why mankind never lives entirely in the present.

The obligatory instinctual transformation subsequent to renunciation

In "Thoughts for the times on war and death" (Freud, 1915b), Freud considered susceptibility to culture, which involves an inborn part and another acquired part, to be grounded in the instinctual transformation that would condition and determine the emergence of cultural hypocrisy on both the individual and the collective level.

Indeed, subject to the influence of education and the environment, *we can conduct ourselves well in the cultural sense* without the essential transformation of selfish instincts into social instincts having taken place. Responding exclusively to social demands, our cultural behaviour simply provides selfish benefits.

Moreover, in *Three Essays on the Theory of Sexuality*, Freud considered that the organisation of human sexual development into two phases, those of childhood and of puberty, separated by the latency stage, represented "one of the conditions of the aptitude of men to developing a higher civilization, but also of their tendency to neurosis" (Freud, 1905d, p. 234).

Indeed, "in the space of a few years the little primitive creature must turn into a civilized human being" (Freud, 1940a, p. 185), meaning that he or she will have had to take a major shortcut to traverse a quite long portion of the development of human culture so as later to become "what we call a normal man, the bearer and in part the victim, of the civilization that has been so painfully acquired" (Freud, 1910a, p. 36). This is precisely the object of *Kulturarbeit* for every human child or, expressed in another way, *the task of education* which, according to Freud, is representative of the "cultural demands in the family" and would be sustained by the child's playing, guided especially by the desire to grow up and be an adult.

Acting upon the sexual instinct and upon the aggressive instinct, this instinctual transformation–reorganisation necessarily active throughout each person's life is put in place during "ontogenesis", which according to Freud would be "organically determined and fixed by heredity" (Freud, 1905d, p. 177).

After the programmed "dissolution of the Oedipus complex" (Freud, 1924d), because of the threat of castration (in boys), it would be characterised by:

- The repression of infantile sexuality accompanied by its major reaction-formations, which are disgust, shame, pity, morality, as well as the barring of incest, but also those connected with anal eroticism (order and cleanliness) so important for culture and contributing to the formation of character.

- Aim-inhibition expressed by feelings of tenderness for family and friends.
- The establishment and development of the work of sublimation of the ego, which will be considered later on.
- The development of feelings of identification, both parental ones constituting the nucleus of the superego and ones involving the formation of the character of the ego playing a role in the construction of a post-oedipal sexual identity.
- The limiting of narcissism, and the development of object-love, the transformation of selfish impulses into social instincts by adding erotic components of a homosexual nature.
- The twofold reversal of instinct, in particular of sadism into masochism, would be clearly favoured by *Kulturarbeit*. These sadistic instincts may also be subject to other socially acceptable fates. In particular, their sublimation associated with the energy of scopic pleasure would be at the origin of the instinct to know.
- Finally, the "instinct of destruction, moderated and tamed, and, as it were, inhibited in its aim, must, when it is directed towards objects, provide the ego with the satisfaction of its vital needs and with control over nature" (Freud, 1930a, p. 121).

Freud nevertheless detected *a difference between the sexes, especially as concerns the building up of the reaction-formations of the latency stage and the structuration of the superego.*

In *Three Essays on the Theory of Sexuality* (Freud, 1905d), he noted that this building up takes place earlier in a little girl, and encounters less resistance in her, than in a boy, just as engaging in the repression process seems greater, or of greater significance. Moreover, when manifesting themselves, partial sexual instincts prefer to take a passive form. On the other hand, the auto-eroticism of the erogenous zones would be the same in both sexes, hence the absence of sexual difference in childhood.

Later, with regard to the superego, Freud pointed out to us that in girls, their distinct structuration leads to a different level of morality. The "switching off" of the castration anxiety would be replaced by another form of anxiety, that of loss of love-object dependent on external conditions. And, Freud reminded, "the super-ego is never so inexorable, so impersonal, so independent of its emotional origins as when we require it in men" (Freud, 1925j, p. 257).

Around the age of eleven years, with the advent of that flood tide of sexual need, it, in fact, finds in these reaction-formations dykes that prescribe for it outlets called normal and make it impossible for it to revive the perverse instincts subjected to repression.

The ban on incest having been established during the latency stage, parents can perform their task, which is to guide their pubescent child in the choice of the sexual object that will exclude them as primary love-objects and will be oriented towards strangers. At the same time that they overcome and reject their plainly incestuous phantasies, adolescents must accomplish, Freud tells us, "one of the most significant, but also one of the most painful, psychical achievements of the pubertal period . . . detachment from parental authority, a process that alone makes possible the opposition, which is so important for the progress of civilization, between the new generation and the old" (Freud, 1905d, p. 227). For every adolescent, this detachment from the family becomes a task that society often helps him or her solve by means of puberty and initiation rites, explained Freud in *Civilization and Its Discontents* (Freud, 1930a, p. 103).

On the socialisation of the individual

This work of instinctual transformation–reorganisation would determine every individual's conditions of socialisation. This process would also involve each one's "socialization of sexuality", meaning, the acquisition of a genital sexuality in the service of reproduction, having subordinated pregenital instincts and involving a convergence towards the same goal and object of flows of tenderness and sensuality during puberty. This socialised sexuality said to be normal would cause culture to progress, affirmed Freud, in " 'Civilized' sexual morality and modern nervous illness" (Freud, 1908d). Moreover, one would find aim-inhibition and sublimation of the homosexual libido at work contributing to the establishment of lasting social bonds, friendship, the formation of social feelings based on identifications stemming from reaction-formations against hostile and jealous impulses, a substitution of ideal cultural objects for each person's ego ideal, thus a prevailing of objectality over narcissism in the individual libidinal economy. Indeed, within society, the curtailment of narcissism—therefore, of singularities—to the benefit of similarities and object-love could only inhibit the hostile impulses arising out of narcissistic self-assertion intolerant of the slightest difference that could then find satisfaction outside the society in question, which indicated to Freud that object-love is a factor favouring culture.

What can now be said of the role of sublimation in this process of the individual's "incorporation into society"?

This social, non-sexual, fate, of pregenital instincts immediately fits in at the boundary line between two realities—intrapsychic-individual and collective, socio-cultural—realising then the transition and essential connection between one to the other. Several of Freud's texts attest to this. For instance, in *Three Essays on the Theory of Sexuality* (Freud, 1905d) and " 'Civilized' sexual morality and modern nervous illness" (Freud, 1908d), he accorded "cultural value" to the capacity to change the aim of the sexual instinct.

In *From the History of an Infantile Neurosis* (Freud, 1918b), religion is viewed within the context of the education of the individual, both owing to a taming of sexual impulses, which are deviated through sublimation toward spiritual processes offering another form of satisfaction, and owing to the openness to the social relations it offers to the believer, thus enabling all children to achieve the necessary detachment from their families.

In *Civilization and Its Discontents* (Freud, 1930a), Freud established particularly interesting connections among sublimation, work, libidinal economy, and social integration in every individual. He, in fact, presented professional work as a sublimational activity procuring psychical benefits and also determining a primordial condition of the social existence of every subject, something that, moreover, raises questions regarding the limits of the social field of sublimations.

The work of sublimation would thus consist of psychical work accomplished by the ego of every subject experiencing the double pressure of the superego and of culture. Both individual and collective, it consists of a process of derivation, after desexualisation, of perverse sexual instincts from their initial aim towards aims that are non-sexual, socio-cultural, but nevertheless "psychically related to the former". These new aims and objects concern social activities, cultural products—material as well as ideological, scientific, artistic—contributing to the life of the said culture, this symbolic universe enveloping and unifying every human community.

Inspired by Freud, who tried to define the concept of instinct, I would say that regarding its individual pole, Kulturarbeit is the psychical work required of all individuals by culture relayed and supported by the superego, with a view to connecting them to social realities, meaning to incorporating them into society, therefore to their participation in culture.

Some remarks and reflections

- *I have observed circularity existing between the two poles, individual and collective, of Kulturarbeit,* accounting for the co-production of individuals and society, as well as the necessary transmission of its cultural components, which only exist and are transmitted by its members.

- *In the course of my research, two essential processes of Kulturarbeit, in both the social and the individual field, have become clearly apparent to me: inhibition and symbolisation*—the latter, not pointed out by Freud and, moreover, non-conceptualised—quite obviously referring to the different modes and forms of expression of inhibitions and symbolisations, both individual and collective. How do they connect with sublimation? That is matter calling for investigation.

- *What connections can be established between Kulturarbeit and dream work, but also between Kulturarbeit and the "work of the negative" as conceptualised by André Green* (Green, 1993), in which we find certain processes of "instinctual negativation" as well as those of identification?

Through its modes of distorting unconscious wishes and thoughts, and subject to the pressure of censorship, would dream-work be a model?

Often concerned about establishing connections between individual and collective fields, Freud asked,

> Where can we find a similar distortion of a psychical act in social life? Only where two persons are concerned, one of whom possesses a certain degree of power which the second is obliged to take into account. In such a case the second person will distort his psychical acts or, as we might put it, will dissimulate. The politeness which I practise every day is to a large extent dissimulation of this kind. (Freud, 1900a, pp. 141–142)

The same is the case with the political writer who has hostile truths to express in opposition to the powers that be, but must also fear social censorship. This is one of the manifestations of *Kulturarbeit*: dissimulation, inhibition, even reversal of the affects leading to another form of *social hypocrisy*.

In addition, let me mention the "secondary elaboration" of dream content accomplished by the ego, which according to Freud would be the *prototype* of all formations of systems or "world views" like animism, religion, philosophy, even science. However, *prototype* implies a set of transformations carried out in the socio-cultural field in accordance with processes other than those of the individual psyche.

- Reading *Moses and Monotheism* affords a glimpse into the accomplishment of a paradigmatic instance of *Kulturarbeit*: Moses' creation of the Jewish people, with their psychical, physical, and socio-cultural identity characteristics connecting with their unique history, how a founder of a religion, in fact, *invents* the identity of a people through a religious ideology that will therefore organise them, both on the collective plane and within its members themselves. Thus, religion, component and basic category of "culture in itself", would also participate in the structuring of the psyche of those participating in it. But in what ways?

- *If the essential goal of Kulturarbeit, as well as of Eros, seems to me to be the creation of multiple psychical, psychosocial, and social ties, to be noted is the frequent, even quasi-permanent, existence of situations of undoing of ties even of excessive ties, therefore, of failures of Kulturarbeit, on both the individual and social level,* very probably proceeding from vicissitudes in the shifting, unstable balance of forces of linking–integration (Eros) and undoing–disintegration (instincts of destruction) within individuals and society.

Thus, these failures of *Kulturarbeit* can be conceived of as, on the one hand, *pathological social products*, like war and other regressive collective manifestations and, on the other hand, *as individual pathological productions*.

Let us take a look at these pathological social products

Regarding this, Freud brought up a specific feature of psychical development for which every earlier stage of development persists alongside the later stage that has arisen from it. So, silent for an indeterminate amount of time, that earlier psychical state can manifest itself and then become the sole form of expression of psychical forces, therefore, cancelling out the forms that have undergone further evolution. He wrote of the "extraordinary plasticity of mental developments" characterised by their capacity for "involution-regression" (Freud, 1915b, p. 285–286). This is the case of war as a social phenomenon with its impact on the regressive behaviour of individuals, something that suggests a new analogy between individual and group psychology.

Thus, in "Thoughts for the times on war and death", Freud presented war as placing itself above "all the restrictions ... which in peace-time the states had bound themselves to observe" (Freud, 1915b, 278–279) and breaking "all the common bonds between the contending peoples" (Freud, 1915b, p. 279). It attests to the "low morality" (Freud, 1915b, p. 280) of the states in external relations and the brutality in the behaviour of individuals. Indeed, the influences of war figure among the powers capable of producing involution, that is to say, of undoing the instinctual transformation upon which our "susceptibility to culture" rests.

It actually "strips us of the later accretions of civilization, and lays bare the primal man" (Freud, 1915b, p. 299).

Then in "Why war?", Freud explained that "a lust for aggression and destruction" certainly counts among the motives inciting human beings to war. He wrote of how "the countless cruelties in history and in our everyday lives vouch for its existence and its strength. The satisfaction of these destructive impulses is of course facilitated by their admixture with others of an erotic and idealistic kind" (Freud, 1933b, p. 210).

Nevertheless, Freud considered that wars could establish large units within which a strong central power capable of preventing new wars could be created. Indeed, he observed that wars have not disappeared and, moreover, large-scale wars have replaced numerous small wars (Freud, 1933b, p. 207).

- What about other forms of collective violence, those of criminality, but also suicide, as a social phenomenon?
- As well as evidence of failures in the work of inter- and transgenerational psychical transmission and that of cultural heritage?
- What about situations of collective turmoil, social hyper-cohesiveness in which each person's individual identity recedes into the

background in favour of the community forming an "imaginary common body" (Anzieu, 1984) constituted by strong narcissistic identifications borne by a common ideal? It is a matter of religious, political events especially.

- In addition, if cultural and individual developments work with similar means (*Kulturarbeit*), and if cultural tendencies condition the breaking out of individual neuroses, why not imagine, according to Freud, that it might not be the same for socio-cultural communities, even for the whole of humanity, hence his hypothesis in *Civilization and Its Discontents* concerning the possible existence of collective, or social, or communal neuroses. Notwithstanding, he warns us about the methodological danger of extending these analogies, meaning, of taking human beings and concepts out of their original context and development (Freud, 1930a, p. 144).

The individual psychopathological products favoured and/or induced by cultural demands and pathogenic social circumstances

- In " 'Civilized' sexual morality and modern nervous illness" (Freud, 1908d), Freud already mentioned the *elusive, asocial nature of neuroses*, the symptoms of which procure substitutive satisfaction, then in "The psychoanalytic view of psychogenic disturbance of vision", the latter would be characterised as "ways in which these processes of transformation in the sexual component instincts may miscarry" (Freud, 1910i, p. 215).
- He also discussed the *disruption of the relation to reality* and the attempts to replace it observed in neurosis and psychosis (Freud, 1924e, p. 187).

Neuroses and psychoses are born out of the ego's conflicts with its diverse dominant instances, therefore, correspond to a *failure in the functioning of the ego* in its efforts to reconcile all diverse demands with one another.

- *Sexual perversions*, failures in libidinal development barring access to genital sexuality thus prove to be inhibitions, on the one hand, dissociations in sexual development, on the other. Freud described them as a failure of individual *Kulturarbeit* with regard to the necessary socio-cultural building up of "barriers", therefore of limits, circumscribing the field of a possible, non-dangerous, adult human sexuality, and in addition bringing about cultural progress.

• *Homosexuality*. Apart from its belonging to the "bad uses of sexuality" identified by anthropologists, in "Some neurotic mechanisms in jealousy, paranoia and homosexuality", Freud particularly inquired into its connection with social feeling. He wrote that "In the light of psycho-analysis, we are accustomed to regard social feeling as a sublimation of homosexual attitudes towards objects. In the homosexuals with marked social interests, it would seem that the detachment of social feeling from object-choice has not been fully carried through" (Freud, 1922b, p. 232).

• *Criminals*, especially out of a sense of guilt (Freud, 1916d). Among adult criminals, Freud distinguished between those who commit crimes without any sense of guilt—with a lack of moral inhibition, and in a fight against society—from those, representing the majority, who are filled with a sense of unconscious guilt and for whom, according to him, penal codes are established. Psycho-analysis discovered that such criminal acts had mainly been committed because they were prohibited and that for their doers mental relief was associated with performing them. They, in fact, suffered from an oppressive feeling of guilt whose origin was unknown to them, but which was correlative to repressed oedipal desires. And after having committed a misdeed, that oppression was mitigated, relieved by being able to attach that feeling something real and actual (Freud, 1916d, p. 332).

• *Further inquiry into suicide as another form of failure of individual Kulturarbeit should also be undertaken.*

• *Finally, what about Kulturarbeit, both individual and collective, in the "emergency experimental situations" represented by the "borderline experiences" that human beings may face or may have faced?*

In her remarkable work *De la guérison psychanalytique*, Nathalie Zaltzman explains that this inevitable borderline experience that a human being cannot overcome without suffering mortal injury can be produced by an extreme natural physical environment, but can also be the product of a socio-political environment in a destructive total-itarianism, the extreme example of which is that of the concentration and extermination camps. It may also be the work of an individual mental relation (Zaltzman, 1998, p. 138).

Introduction to a critical discussion, or Kulturarbeit *and the socio-anthropological corpus*

A critical discussion of the notion of *Kulturarbeit* is called for. It could inquire, in particular, into its heuristic value for both the psychoana-lytical theoretical corpus and the socio-anthropological corpus. It would necessarily be backed up by the writings of anthropologists and post-Freudian scholars.

I initiated this discussion in my book entitled *Le Complexe d'Œdipe, cristallisateur du débat psychanalyse/anthropologie* (Smadja, 2009), which takes a twofold approach, historical and epistemological, to exploring the conflictual relationships between those two sciences. I suggested that if, in the manner of the symbolic since Marcel Mauss (Mauss, 1924), the unconscious is a unifying factor in the human sciences, therefore connects anthropology and psycho-analysis, culture also proves to be another common object to be shared scientifically. Indeed, both enjoy a twofold status, individual and collective, intrapsychical and physical, as well as historical and socio-cultural. If the uncon-scious manifests itself in historical and socio-cultural reality through a collective organisation of its processes and its formations differing from those present in every subject and to be explored, culture is also an intrapsychical and physical reality present in each individual, therefore, in each of the members of a given society, through the agen-cies of the ego, superego, and ego ideal, but also through the multiple forms of bodily marking, bodily practices, and techniques. This indi-vidual experience, product of the enculturation process or of "socio-cultural introjection", as I myself have formulated it, is a condition for both the humanisation and socialisation of every human being and for the production, preservation, transmission, and reproduction of every society.

Thus, through their first common object, human beings, psycho-analysis and anthropology, in fact, share two major attributes of the humanity of human beings: the unconscious and culture.

So, it seems to me that, as I have explained it, the Freudian notion of *Kulturarbeit* particularly takes into account the complex dialectical nature of relations between the unconscious and culture in both the individual and the collective space, in other words, the relationships between individual and collective realities in terms of the dynamic and antagonistic relationships of mutual interpenetration and inter-dependency. Consequently, I am revealing *its nature and interdisciplinary dimension* concealed from us up until this point and henceforth essential. *This is why I propose to confer a new status upon it, that of interdisciplinary concept, the significance of which will have to be assessed in the field of the human and social sciences. This concept of Kulturarbeit could ultimately promote fruitful collaboration between psychoanalysts and other specialists in the human sciences.*

Moreover, certain sociologists and anthropologists have introduced more or less related concepts.

Among the sociologists may be cited a major figure, Norbert Elias (Elias, 1939), and his concept of "civilizing process", a technical term belonging to the sociology of history and a tool for the description and analysis of long-term social processes. It takes into account the close historical interdependency between social structures, ways of exercising power, and psychical structures or "habitus".

Both individual and collective, this *civilising process* is principally characterised by the transformation of norms of sensitivity and behaviours, by the internalisation of external constraints into self-constraint, by attaining mastery over affects correlative to the formation of a superego, characteristic of the "psychical habitus" of every civilised individual or the "personality structure" of "civilized" people, and all of that standing in a relationship of interdependency and correspondence with the social structures and sociogenesis of the State.

This civilising process is oriented "towards the stronger and more complete 'intimization', especially of all bodily functions, towards their enclosure in particular enclaves" (Elias, 1939, p. 159), increasingly leading to the split between the aspects of human life that can find expression in social relationships and those that must be saved for one's private life. Two spheres of human life then become divided, one intimate, secret, the other public, open, on display (Elias, 1939, p. 159).

As a consequence of this behavioural split, certain actions being permitted in public, others prohibited, the human psychical structure is also modified, notably towards the creation of internal splits. Indeed, one of the consequences of this civilising process would be the emergence of consciousness of oneself as separate from others and from society, that of an "ego", of "something repressed", of a "super-ego", as well as the elaboration of the concept of the individual and of the individual–society conflict (Elias, 1939, p, 416).

Apart from civilising bodily functions, Elias discussed civilising table manners, as well as other sectors of "civilization": relationships between the sexes, sexual relationships and marriage, parenthood, and aggression, in particular.

In addition, Elias proposed interpreting these correspondences between the structures of the individual personality and social structures not only in terms of the socialisation of the individual—in the sense that, human beings who go from one group to another undergo changes in their individuality throughout their lives, something that does not, therefore, exclusively concern children and adolescents—but also in terms of individualisation of social phenomena, a process that is both dialectically opposed and complementary, consisting in an internalisation of socio-cultural components.

In *Au-delà de Freud: Sociologie, psychologie, psychanalyse*, Elias wrote that not only realities like the standard language of a society, but also the common store of knowledge, the common social norms for behaviour, and many other of society's forms of expression, only exist by becoming the property of their individual members, only by being a part of themselves, poured into more or less individualised moulds. Thought, speech, or writing are examples of this. In any era, these activities all bear a specific social imprint that is at the same time expressed in a more or less individualised form (Elias, 1990, p. 77). This is a particularly Durkheimian idea. Anthropologists call this process "enculturation", and I use the expression "cultural introjection" correlative to the process of incorporation into society. As it happens, the individual pole of *Kulturarbeit* accounts for this.

Among anthropologists, Françoise Héritier, her idea of "symbolic work" in particular, deserves mention (Héritier, 1996).

According to her, placed in the natural environment, a place of observation of the difference between the sexes, of the procreative relation, with the idea of a circulation, even of an exchange, of bodily fluids to another person (sperm, placenta), the body represents the first object of reflection by human beings and constitutes the founding substrate of the first categories of symbolic thought, those of the identical and the different. Difference would be expressed in contrasts or binary categories, the first pair of which, masculine–feminine, subject to hierarchical ranking (masculine > feminine), functions as a paradigm in relation to the others. Based upon this universal given would be a creation of social institutions and of representation and thought systems, that is to say, of an "ideological body", therefore of a symbolic order.

Thus, kinship systems, as well as the multiple manifestations of the differential valence of the sexes, like the discourse on sterility, represent good examples of symbolic work. According to her, every kinship system is, therefore, led to deal conceptually with the same elementary biological data, which are universal. A kinship system is not the expression of pure biological facts of reproduction, but necessarily takes basic biological data into account (Héritier, 1996, p. 56).

The notion of "work of culture" of the American anthropologist of Sri Lankan origin, Gananath Obeyesekere endeavours to account for the manner in which "unconscious infantile motivations" are transformed into symbolic forms, be they personal symbols, myths, or collective images. Thus, a pre-established cultural system of symbols would enable individuals to express and control their unconscious psychical conflicts of infantile origin. When used, these symbols, laden with meaning, will be comprehensible to members of society within a specific cultural context. The model for this work would be dream work, with its processes of transformation of unconscious infantile motivations into dream images and symbols. Obeyesekere then conceives of the dream as "a symbolic set" (Obeyesekere, 1990). However, dreams are not culture.

Inspired by Obeyesekere, Bernard Juillerat (Juillerat, 1993), has taken up this notion of *Kulturarbeit* to explore the processes of transformations and mediations of unconscious phantasies into cultural symbols elaborated by the collective imagination. This work would involve three types of processes: primary, secondary processes, and a process of socio-cultural elaboration, a sort of collective, historical secondary process tied to external factors (natural milieu, social norms, and cultural values, events . . .).

Then, the notion of "anthropopoïesis" introduced by a group of anthropologists (F. Affergan, C. Calame, U. Fabietti, M. Kilani, and F. Remotti) in their collective work entitled *Figures de l'humain* (Affergan et al., 2003), which they define both as "renaissance" of human beings as social beings (anthropo-genesis) and as process of invention of "models and fictions of humanity". Indeed, human beings' existence precedes their essence, which is to *invent* and can only be constituted collectively in interaction with human beings through a never definitive historical process, but also through the intermediary of different institutional and ritual constraints in accordance with normative models often elaborated, symbolised, and transformed into traditions in genealogical accounts. Thus, by inventing culture and society, people above all give birth to human reality.

Finally, let us finish our review with the notion of "production of society" elaborated by Maurice Godelier (Godelier, 2004, p. 317).

Human beings live in societies, but also produce society in order to live, that is to say that they have the capacity to modify their forms of social existence by transforming their relationships (kinship, political, economic, religious) among themselves and with nature. "By producing an increasing portion of their material and social conditions of existence, humans are the only animal species that has become co-responsible, with nature, for its own evolution" (Godelier, 2004, p. 468). "And among actions humans undertook on themselves, in the forefront stands the control and management of their sexuality. In effect, humans are the only animal species that consciously and socially 'manages' its sexuality, that explicitly, in the form of oral and/or written laws, establishes prohibitions and limits on certain uses people can make of their sexual organs", for example, incest, necrophilia, and zoophilia (Godelier, 2004, p. 469).

According to him, since the social order is not only moral and sexual, but also cosmic, most of the time the reasons appealed to for these sexual prohibitions are at once social, moral, and religious ("cosmic"), that is to say, both real and imaginary. These imaginary explanations, objects of shared collective beliefs, are interpretations of social reality, therefore, a matter of "ideal" reality, existing only in thought and through collective thought, but also produce social reality through their crystallisation in institutions and staging in symbolic practices, rituals, validating and legitimising these collective representations in return. However, Godelier considered that there is a measure of arbitrariness in this collective imaginary production (Godelier, 2004, p. 312).

All said and done, apart from Elias, we see that each of the anthropologists and sociologists has inquired into aspects taken into consideration in the notion in question without tackling its very rich and complex dialectical dimension. I shall plan to pursue this investigation within the socio-anthropological literature in an upcoming work.

By way of conclusion

Having come to the end of my exploratory investigation of Freudian depictions of society and culture, both of these notions often being used interchangeably, what might I say about it?

In the first place, society and culture prove to be omnipresent and omnipotent for us, both in psychoanalysis and in Freud's life's work, in particular through "reality" and the "external world", terms belonging to metapsychological language, on the basis of which the ego is differentiated from the id of every individual and, correlatively, the substitution of the reality principle for the pleasure principle effected what Freud considered to be a "psychic revolution" leading to the transformation of the pleasure-ego into a reality-ego. These expressions principally designate socio-cultural reality and less frequently nature or material reality. Society and culture are the sources and places of "external real necessity", of the "power of the present", of constraints, demands, and "failure to provide satisfaction", but also of drive satisfaction and of actions, particularly aiming at adaptations, modifications, even mastery and sought-after satisfaction. From that point on, they will compel each person to engage in ongoing psychic work throughout his or her entire life.

Furthermore, in the course of his writings, Freud presented us with *evolving personal conceptions*, independent of the theorising of the sociologists and anthropologists who were his contemporaries. It is a matter of socio-anthropology that is *psychoanalytic in essence*, both through its epistemological foundations, its method, and through its conceptual language, which fails to take into account the distinctiveness of the functioning and the singular products of this *other reality*, which is just as complex as psychic reality, systemic and symbolic in nature, and riddled with multiple antagonisms. However, in other respects, Freudian thought reveals itself to be a product of historically and social-culturally determined thought that shows evidence of certain social and ideological representations prevalent in his time, but also in Viennese society undergoing a serious crisis. Let me indicate, in particular, the radical antagonism between individual and society, as well as the evolutionist ideology, in its developmental version (the development of society is comparable to that of an individual) and progressive version (evolution is animated by the progress sustained by the triumph of reason, dogma prevailing during the nineteenth century and appropriated by the liberal bourgeois members of *his* society).

So it is that I have detected an evolving progression of his discourse inherent in the very evolution of psychoanalytic doctrine, be it the theory of drives or of the psychic apparatus, for example.

This is why, I shall distinguish between two periods:

- That of the first topic, with some major texts, including: *Three Essays on the Theory of Sexuality* (Freud, 1905d), " 'Civilized' sexual morality and modern nervous illness" (Freud, 1908d), and *Totem and Taboo* (Freud, 1912–1913).
- That of the second topic, dominated by three texts, but to which I shall add a fourth, "A short account of psychoanalysis" (Freud, 1924f), *The Future of an Illusion* (Freud, 1927c), *Civilization and Its Discontents* (Freud, 1930a), and *Moses and Monotheism* (Freud, 1939a).

The first period

Very early on, Freud defended the thesis of the *libidinal drive foundations* of culture that he would later define as his "psychic capital", which is not very surprising for a psychoanalyst unaware of socio-anthropological theorisations! Indeed, as early as the *Three Essays on the Theory of Sexuality* (Freud, 1905d), cultural productions are a matter of acquired sexual components, forces of sexual drives diverted from their sexual aim and directed towards new, non-sexual aims, through the process of sublimation, individual as well as collective. In so doing, he affirmed, on the one hand, that this process participates in the constitution of culture and, on the other hand, that it is a matter of production that is collective through the participation of each of its members. Consequently, these drive components, sublimated or inhibited, even repressed, with respect to their aim, objects of forms of renunciation and refashioning, represent the "culture's psychic capital", which must necessarily take a great quantity of psychic energy away from the sexuality of its participants for its own needs of consumption. This economic, drive approach of culture is also particularly manifest in " 'Civilized' sexual morality and modern nervous illness" (Freud, 1908d). While a culture is generally built upon the repression of drives, it is also a question of each person's personal gift of a part of his or her drive capital, libidinal and hostile motions, which will, therefore, represent every individual's contribution to the constitution of this "common cultural property in material and ideal goods", as a genuine participant in the constitution of the culture in question, which is a *collective enterprise and common property*. This very notion of "common cultural property" would be neglected during the second period. In addition, he emphasised that *through the repression and displacement of drives, normal sexuality would bring the culture to advance*, in contrast to the perverse deviations in conflict with it through their incapacity to mobilise these sexual components. Moreover, Freud plainly states that a drive's "cultural value" lies in its capacity for displacement of the object and aim.

In *Totem and Taboo*, through analogy with the neurotic symptomatic formations, the primordial institutions have an "animal" origin in drives. They appertain to drive conflicts in the species that are oedipal in nature and constitute compromise social solutions to the problem of wish compensation. Realised collectively, they represent "goods of humanity".

But above all, Freud's method led him to set up the ambivalent paternal side of the Oedipus complex at the foundation of culture, then as an agent of liaison between the two fields—intrapsychic-individual and collective, socio-cultural—from a certain number of needs, capacities, and processes of human mental activity, but also taking into consideration an essential analogy between the individual and society, that of a psyche—individual, in the former case, and mass in the latter case—within which we inevitably find similar processes. Individual psyche and culture are correlative, therefore interdependent.

Finally, the introduction of the notion of a "mass psyche" ensuring the continuity of psychic life between the generations is an extension of Wundt's notion of collective psyche as an extension of the individual psyche. It displays similarities with that of "collective consciousness" introduced by Durkheim (Durkheim, 1893). As I have already formulated it, it pertains to the culture and represents an instance of it by referring to "human mental activity". It does not stand in a relationship of identity with the individual psyche, as group psychoanalysts have shown well, contrary to what Freud had imagined. In fact, its processes and its formations are distinctive of it, even though some analogies exist between these two psychic realities: individual and collective.

The second period

Freud's "A short account of psychoanalysis" (Freud, 1924f) presents culture as the domain of expression of "human mental activity", presupposing a projective activity of external "shaping" of an internal world involving three portions corresponding to three areas of its representation of culture:

- Combat with reality, nature, determining a community of work and interests of libidinously linked human beings, and a correlative social life.
- The substitutive satisfactions of repressed wishes, figuring among them myths, literary and artistic creations.
- The major institutions that enable mastery of the Oedipus complex and the individual libido's transition from its infantile liaisons to wished for social liaisons.

Then, with *The Future of an Illusion* (Freud, 1927c) and *Civilization and Its Discontents* (Freud, 1930a), Freud plunges us into an elaborate description and exposes us to some structural antagonisms between culture or society and its members, as well as to paradoxes intrinsic to the culture or society itself.

First of all, he paints a picture for us of the overall culture involving, once again, three areas:

1. The *material aspects* proceeding from two types of activities, those that are useful, vital in nature, enabling the acquisition and fabrication of goods and referring to the "material culture", and those that are useless, but nevertheless necessary to human beings, among them beauty, order, and cleanliness.
2. The *"intellectual" aspects* or *"psychic goods"* integrating religious systems, philosophical speculation, artistic creations, as well as the formations of ideal or store of mankind's cultural ideals, and the human superego as "psychological cultural capital".
3. Finally, what pertains to *modes of regulating social relations* ensured by ethics or morality, one of the expressions of the cultural superego, Freud would point out to us in *Civilization and Its Discontents*, which produces its ideals and raises its demands.

What are its principal antagonisms and paradoxes that are the source of conflicts and of ambivalence with regard to it?

The nature–culture antagonism

If the true foundation of the existence of culture, which blends in with its principal task, consists of a community of work and human interests associated together by identifications, aim-inhibited relations, and sublimated homosexual bonds, *essentially aiming at protecting them from the dangers of nature* and at dominating it in order to obtain vital goods, then it is also a *source of multiple forms of suffering* by the determining of a twofold coercion to work, both psychic (sublimational, for example) and social, individual, and collective, and by the instinctual renunciation required, therefore engendering sacrifices.

The individual–society-culture antagonism

But, it is also threatened from within by another source of danger: it must protect itself from its participants, human individuals endowed with "drives of animal origin", therefore, with what are called antisocial drives, sexual as well as destructive, that make virtual enemies of them, not to mention their narcissism, which must be held in check and changed into love of object, hence love as a factor of culture.

Freud ultimately identified two sources of hostility of individuals from which culture must protect itself:

- That inherent in the *animal nature* of human beings, constituted of "selfish", sexual and destructive, anti-social and anti-cultural drives, in search of satisfaction, and confronted with privations established by the basic prohibitions.
- That determined by the constraint to individual and collective work and the requisite drive renunciation, which engenders psychic sacrifices in its participants, determining a position virtually hostile to culture and its demands.

Its modalities of protection are also multiple. It must compensate those participating in it for the sacrifices of drive it imposes on them by offering them "psychic goods", in fact, having this purpose, according to Freud, just like the institutions, devices, and commandments.

Nevertheless, culture's most determinant and meaningful method of protection against its participants' destruction drive—the most dangerous one—would be considered the establishment of the superego or conscience in each individual, thus becoming a "vehicle of culture", and the correlative advent of a sense of guilt. Culture, work of Eros and serving it, goes hand in hand with this feeling of guilt, which inevitably induces a loss of happiness. This is the very purpose of *Kulturarbeit*, in both its individual and collective field.

For each society, it will, therefore, be a matter of finding modes of balancing these two sorts of demands: individual and collective.

Among the other "socio-cultural" antagonisms that I have detected, I would like to indicate:

- That between women, as representing the interests of the family and of sexual life, and the culture.
- That between the family, from which young people must break away, helped in this task by the rites of puberty instituted by the society, and the culture.

- That between men and women in their relationship to the culture and to *Kulturarbeit*.
- That between *Kulturarbeit* and sexuality, through the necessary work of drive sublimation, which impoverishes the erotic drive capital and its dangers of drive defusion.
- That between homosexual ties that are sublimated and inhibited with respect to the goal prevailing within the community of work and human interests and the heterosexuality of conjugal bonds.
- That between sexuality as an autonomous source of pleasure and marriage.

Society would impose upon all its members the same kind of genital sexual life based on a choice of one heterosexual object—therefore ruling out multiplicity of choice, the homosexual object and perversions—and a relationship between one man and one woman, principally procreative and indissoluble, within the framework of the institution of marriage.

But Freud also proposed a dynamic vision of culture as "process", work of Eros that *urges* human beings *to bond libidinally* among themselves in order to form great social units, all the while being subject to Ananke, real necessity, therefore, external reality. Consequently, Eros and Ananke are the parents of human culture. This process develops on the scale of humanity and seems analogous to individual development and to organic processes. Indeed, having to confront a major obstacle, the destructive instinct, it will, therefore, be a matter of a combat animated by necessary movements of fusion–defusion–refusion between Eros and this destructive instinct, corresponding thus to the essential content of life.

In *Moses and Monotheism*, Freud reminds us that at work in the psychic life of the individual, are not only *contents experienced by himself or herself*, but also *innate contents*, "memory traces bound to an experience lived by earlier generations" continuing to persist as elements of phylogenetic origin and constituting an *archaic heritage*. For Freud, this notion of archaic heritage seems to represent *an agent of liaison between phylogenesis and ontogenesis*, as well as individual and collective psychologies.

Moreover, if the foundations of the culture condition and favour, through the constraint of drive restrictions in particular, the outbreak of neurosis in its participants, and if the analogy between cultural development and that of the individual particularly based on certain similar processes presents a value, Freud allows himself to infer the possible existence of *neurotic* cultures and cultural eras under the influence "of tendencies of culture". Thus, culture produces individual neurosis, but also collective neurosis.

As for the Freudian notion of *Kulturarbeit*, it runs through all of Freud's work, from the *Interpretation of Dreams* on, even if it is not often designated as such. As I have identified it, this notion expresses the existence of relationships of interdependency and interpenetration between socio-cultural and psychic and bodily individual realities. And the originality of Freudian thought is to have indicated to us the diverse modes of leaving its imprint and of individual transmission, bodily as well as intrapsychic, of what is cultural and social, as well as signifying to us that this *introjection of social aspects and of culture* conditions the constitution of a differentiated psychic apparatus, therefore, the psychic hominisation of every individual that would permit his or her socialisation, therefore, his or her incorporation into society, conferring upon him or her the status of "person" or of "subject". Thus, these subjects would participate in the collective work of a social nature, which is productive, preserving, and reproductive for their society and culture, their "common property".

With *methodological impertinence*, Freud would have established some foundations of a necessary psychoanalytic approach to *society* and *culture*, which would be taken up again and developed by other authors from varied perspectives. We may cite, in particular, Geza Roheim, Abram Kardiner, and Georges Devereux. I plan to pursue this exploration in the work of these authors, as well as in that of contemporary authors. Nevertheless, it seems to me urgent, on the one hand, to elaborate a heuristic psychoanalytic methodology, which group psychoanalysts have initiated, on the other hand, to combine, within the framework of pluri- and interdisciplinary collaboration, the (individual and group) psychoanalytic approach to historical as well as sociological, anthropological, and linguistic approaches within *the perspective of a genuinely pertinent and fruitful investigation of the complexity of this human reality.*

REFERENCES

Affergan, F., Borutti, S., Calame, C., Fabietti, U., Kilani, M. & Remotti, F. (Eds.) (2003). *Figures de l'humain*. Paris: EHESS.

Anzieu, D. (1984). *Le groupe et l'unconscient. L'imaginaire groupal* [The Group and the Unconscious]. London: Routledge, 1999.

Assoun, P-L. (1993). *Freud et les sciences sociales*. Paris: Armand Colin.

Bachofen, J. J. (1861). *Das Mutterrecht: eine Untersuchung über die Gynaikokratie der alten Welt nach ihrer religiösen und rechtlichen Natur*. Stuttgart: Verlag von Krais und Hoffmann.

Bastide, R. (1950). *Sociologie et psychanalyse*. Paris: Presses Universitaires de France.

Broca, P. (1871). *Mémoires d'anthropologie* (Vol. 1). Paris: C. Reinwald et Cie.

Bullitt, W. C. (1966). *Thomas Woodrow Wilson, Twentieth-eighth President of the United States*. Boston, MA: Houghton and Mifflin.

Durkheim, E. (1893). *Division of Labor in Society*. New York: Free Press, 1997.

Durkheim, E. (1895). *Rules of Sociological Method*. New York: Free Press, 1982.

Durkheim, E. (1897). *Suicide, a Study in Sociology*. New York: Free Press, 1951.

Durkheim, E. (1912). *Elementary Forms of Religious Life*. Oxford: Oxford University Press, 2001.

Elias, N. (1939). *The Civilizing Process*. Oxford: Blackwell, 1969. [Contains the two volumes *Change in behaviour in the secular upper classes in the west*, pp. 1–182; and *State formation and civilisation*, pp. 183–448. Translation of *Über den Prozess der Zivilisation*, first published in 1939 in two volumes: Volume 1, *Wandlungen ders Verhaltens*; Volume 2, *Wandlungen der Gesellschaft*.]

Elias, N. (1990). *Au-delà de Freud: Sociologie, psychologie, psychanalyse*. Paris: La découverte, 2010.

Freud, S. (1892). Extracts from the Fliess papers. *S.E., 1*. London: Hogarth.

Freud, S. (1893h). On the psychical mechanism of hysterical phenomena. *S.E., 3*. London: Hogarth.

Freud, S. (1894a). The neuro-psychoses of defence. *S.E., 3*. London: Hogarth.

Freud, S. (1895a). *Project for a Scientific Psychology. S.E., 1*. London: Hogarth.

Freud, S. (1895d). *Studies on Hysteria. S.E., 2*. London: Hogarth.

Freud, S. (1898a). Sexuality in the aetiology of the neuroses. *S.E., 3*. London: Hogarth.

Freud, S. (1900a). *The Interpretation of Dreams. S.E., 4, 5*. London: Hogarth.

Freud, S. (1905). Stellungnahme zur Eherechts Enquete. In: *Protokolle der Enquete betreffend die Reform des österreichischen Eherechts* (*vom 27 Jänner bis 24 Februar 1905*) (pp. 76–77). Vienna: Verlage der Kulturpolitischen Gesellschaft, 1905 [Sitzung am 8 Februar 1905].

Freud, S. (1905c). *Jokes and their Relation to the Unconscious. S.E., 8*. London: Hogarth.

Freud, S. (1905d). *Three Essays on the Theory of Sexuality. S.E., 7*. London: Hogarth.

Freud, S. (1907a). Delusions and dreams in Jensen's *Gradiva. S.E., 9*. London: Hogarth.

Freud, S. (1907b). Obsessive actions and religious practices. *S.E., 9*. London: Hogarth.

Freud, S. (1907c). The sexual enlightenment of children (An open letter to Dr M. Fürst). *S.E., 9*. London: Hogarth.

Freud, S. (1908c). On the sexual theories of children. *S.E., 9*. London: Hogarth.

Freud, S. (1908d). "Civilized" sexual morality and modern nervous illness. *S.E., 9*. London: Hogarth.

Freud, S. (1908e). Creative writers and day-dreaming. *S.E., 9*. London: Hogarth.

Freud, S. (1909b). *Analysis of a Phobia in a Five-year-old Boy. S.E., 10*. London: Hogarth.

Freud, S. (1909c). Family romances. *S.E., 9*. London: Hogarth.

Freud, S. (1909d). *Notes Upon a Case of Obsessional Neurosis. S.E., 10.* London: Hogarth.

Freud, S. (1910a). Five lectures on psycho-analysis. *S.E., 11.* London: Hogarth.

Freud, S. (1910e). The antithetical meaning of primal words. *S.E., 11.* London: Hogarth.

Freud, S. (1910i). The psycho-analytic view of psychogenic disturbance of vision. *S.E., 11.* London: Hogarth.

Freud, S. (1911b). Formulations on the two principles of mental functioning. *S.E., 12.* London: Hogarth.

Freud, S. (1911c). *Psycho-analytic Notes on an Autobiographical Account of a case of Paranoia (Dementia paranoides). S.E., 12.* London: Hogarth.

Freud, S. (1912). *A Phylogenetic Fantasy, Overview of the Transference Neuroses.* Cambridge, MA: Belknap Press, 1987. [Translation of *Übersicht der Übertragungs-neurosen, ein bisher unbekanntes Manuskript.*]

Freud, S. (1912c). Types of onset of neurosis. *S.E., 12.* London: Hogarth.

Freud, S. (1912–1913). *Totem and Taboo. S.E., 13.* London: Hogarth.

Freud, S. (1913j). The claims of psycho-analysis to scientific interest. *S.E., 13.* London: Hogarth.

Freud, S. (1914c). On narcissism: an introduction. *S.E., 14.* London: Hogarth.

Freud, S. (1915b). Thoughts for the times on war and death. *S.E., 14.* London: Hogarth.

Freud, S. (1915c). Instincts and their vicissitudes. *S.E., 14.* London: Hogarth.

Freud, S. (1915–1916). *Introductory Lectures on Psycho-Analysis (Parts I and II). S.E., 15.* London: Hogarth.

Freud, S. (1916d). Some character-types met with in the course of psycho-analytic work: criminals from a sense of guilt. *S.E., 14.* London: Hogarth.

Freud, S. (1916–1917). *Introductory Lectures on Psycho-Analysis (Part III). S.E., 16.* London: Hogarth.

Freud, S. (1918b). *From the History of an Infantile Neurosis. S.E., 17.* London: Hogarth.

Freud, S. (1919g). Preface to Reik's ritual: psycho-analytical studies. *S.E., 17.* London: Hogarth.

Freud, S. (1920g). *Beyond the Pleasure Principle. S.E., 18.* London: Hogarth.

Freud, S. (1921c). *Group Psychology and the Analysis of the Ego. S.E., 18.* London: Hogarth.

Freud, S. (1922b). Some neurotic mechanisms in jealousy, paranoia and homosexuality. *S.E., 18.* London: Hogarth.

Freud, S. (1923b). *The Ego and the Id. S.E., 19.* London: Hogarth.

Freud, S. (1924c). The economic problem of masochism. *S.E., 19.* London: Hogarth.

Freud, S. (1924d). The dissolution of the Oedipus complex. *S.E., 19.* London: Hogarth.

Freud, S. (1924e). The loss of reality in neurosis and psychosis. *S.E., 19.* London: Hogarth.

Freud, S. (1924f). A short account of psycho-analysis. *S.E., 19.* London: Hogarth.

Freud, S. (1925d). *An Autobiographical Study. S.E., 20.* London: Hogarth.

Freud, S. (1925e). The resistances to psycho-analysis. *S.E., 19.* London: Hogarth.

Freud, S. (1925j). Some psychical consequences of the anatomical distinction between the sexes. *S.E., 19.* London: Hogarth.

Freud, S. (1926d). *Inhibitions, Symptoms and Anxiety. S.E., 20.* London: Hogarth.

Freud, S. (1926e). The question of lay analysis. *S.E., 20.* London: Hogarth.

Freud, S. (1926f). Psycho-analysis. *S.E., 20.* London: Hogarth.

Freud, S. (1927c). *The Future of an Illusion. S.E., 21.* London: Hogarth.

Freud, S. (1928b). Dostoevsky and parricide. *S.E., 21.* London: Hogarth.

Freud, S. (1930a). *Civilization and Its Discontents. S.E., 21.* London: Hogarth.

Freud, S. (1933a). *New Introductory Lectures on Psycho-analysis. S.E., 22.* London: Hogarth.

Freud, S. (1933b). Why war? *S.E., 22.* London: Hogarth.

Freud, S. (1939a). *Moses and Monotheism. S.E., 23.* London: Hogarth.

Freud, S. (1940a). *An Outline of Psycho-analysis. S.E., 23.* London: Hogarth.

Freud, S. (1942a). Psychopathic characters on the stage. *S.E., 7.* London: Hogarth.

Freud, S. (2010). *Œuvres Complètes, Psychanalyse,* Jean Laplanche (Ed.). Paris: Presses Universitaires de France.

Giraud, C. (1997). *Histoire de la sociologie.* Paris: Presses Universitaires de France.

Godelier, M. (2004). *The Metamorphoses of Kinship.* London: Verso, 2011. [Translation of *Métamorphoses de la parenté.*]

Green, A. (1993). *The Work of the Negative.* London: Free Association, 1999. [Translation of *Le Travail du négatif.*]

Héritier, F. (1996). *Masculin/Féminin. La pensée de la différence.* Paris: Odile Jacob.

Juillerat, B. (1993). *Penser l'imaginaire.* Lausanne: Payot, 2001.

Kaës, R. (Ed.). (1993). *Transmission de la vie psychique entre générations*. Paris: Dunod.

Kilani, M. (2009). *Anthropologie, du local au global*. Paris: Armand Colin.

Laplanche, J. (1989). *Traduire Freud*. Paris: Presses Universitaires de France.

Levi-Strauss, C. (1949). *The Elementary Structures of Kinship*. Boston: Beacon Press, 1969. [Translation of *Les Structures élémentaires de la parenté*.]

Malinowski, B. (1922). *The Argonauts of the Western Pacific*. London: George Routledge & Sons, Ltd.

Malinowski, B. (1927). *Sex and Repression in Savage Society*. London: Routledge, 2001.

Mauss, M. (1924). Une catégorie de l'esprit humain: la notion de personne. In: *Sociologie et anthropologie*. Paris: Presses Universitaires de France, 1950.

Mauss, M. (1950). *Sociologie et anthropologie*. Paris: Presses Universitaires de France.

Mauss, M., & Hubert, H. (1902). A General Theory of Magic. In: R. Brain (Trans.), *Sociologie et anthropologie* (pp. 1-141). London: Routledge and Kegan Paul, 1972.

Morgan, L. H. (1871). *Systems of Consanguinity and Affinity of the Human Family*. Lincoln: University of Nebraska Press, 1977.

Morgan, L. H. (1877). *Ancient Society*. New York: Henry Holt and Co.

Obeyesekere, G. (1990). *The Work of Culture; Symbolic Transformation in Psychoanalysis and Anthropology*. Chicago: University of Chicago Press.

Radcliffe-Brown, A. R. (1922). *The Andaman Islanders*. Cambridge, UK: Cambridge University Press.

Radcliffe-Brown, A. R. (1931). *The Social Organization of Australian Tribes*. Melbourne: Macmillan & Co.

Rank, O. (1912). *The Incest Theme in Literature and Legend*. Baltimore: Johns Hopkins Press, 1991. [Translation of *Das Inzest in Dichtung und Sage*.]

Saussure, F. de (1915). *Course in General Linguistics*. C. Bally & A. Sechehaye (Eds.). Chicago: Open Court, 1998.

Schorske, C. (1980). *Fin-De-Siecle Vienna. Politics and Culture*. New York: Vintage, 1981.

Smadja, E. (1993). *Laughter*. London: College Publications, 2013. [Translation of *Le Rire*.]

Smadja, E. (2009). *Le Complexe d'OEdipe, cristallisateur du débat psychanalyse/ anthropologie*. Paris: Presses Universitaires de France.

Smadja, E. (2013). *Freud et la culture*. Paris: Presses Universitaires de France.

Smith, W. R. (1889). *Lectures on the Religion of the Semites. Fundamental Institutions. First Series*. London: Adam & Charles Black.

Tarot, C. (1999). *De Durkheim à Mauss, l'invention du symbolisme*. Paris: La découverte.

Tönnies, F. (1887).*Community and Society*. Mineola, NY: Dover, 2011. [Translation of *Gemeinschaft und Gesellschaft*.]

Tylor, E. B. (1871). *Primitive Culture: Researches into the Development of Mythology, Philosophy, Religions, Art, and Custom (Vol. 1)*. London: John Murray.

van Gennep, A. (1909). *The Rites of Passage*. Chicago: University of Chicago Press, 1960. [Translation of *Les Rites de Passage*.]

von Ehrenfels, C. (1907). *Sexualethik*. Wiesbaden: J. F. Bergmann.

Weber, M. (1922). *Economy and Society: An Outline of Interpretive Sociology*. Berkeley, CA: University of California Press, 1978.

Wundt, W. (1912). *Elemente der Völkerpsychologie*. Leipzig: Kröner. [Translated as *The Elements of Social Psychology*, E. L. Schaub (Trans.). London: Allen & Unwin, 1916.

Zaltzman, N. (1998). *De la guérison psychanalytique*. Paris: Presses Universitaires de France.

INDEX

of analogies, xii
of belief, 60
of desire, 67, 130
of enjoyment, 82
of hostile impulses, 120
of reflection, 158
of renunciation, 43
of science, 90
of shame, 116
real, 16
social, 97
oedipal, 163
  desires, 154
  post-, 147
  state-of-affairs, 79
Oedipus complex, xii, xiv–xv, 25–26,
  39, 49, 61, 67, 70, 79, 118,
  130–131, 133–134, 138, 145–146,
  155, 163–164
ontogenesis, xiii, xv, 27, 41, 71, 73, 94,
  135, 141, 144, 146, 167

phantasy, 15, 76–77, 79, 131 see also:
  unconscious(ness)
  disguised, 80
  group, 116
  incestuous, 148
  primal, 135, 141
  reality-, 15
  wish-, 80
phenomena, 21, 58–59, 86, 94, 105,
  127, 134, 144
  artistic, 100
  correlative, 48, 137
  hysterical, 40
  libidinal, 41
  of conscience, 70
  of life, 53
  physiological, 72
  principal, 21
  religious, 57–59, 62
  social, xiii, xvii, 61, 84, 87, 152,
    157
phylogenesis, xiii, xv, 27, 41, 46, 67,
  94, 100, 129–130, 135, 141, 167

psyche, xiii, xv, 12, 39, 64, 96, 101,
  131, 144, 151, 164
  collective, 95, 164
  human, xvii
  individual, xiii, 107, 145, 151, 164
  mass, xvi, 53, 107, 164

Radcliffe-Brown, A. R., 93, 97
Rank, O., 79
Ratzel, F., 92
reality, xiii, xv–xvi, 3, 9, 15–17, 39, 48,
  55, 59, 61, 64, 71, 76–78, 87, 94,
  99–100, 104–105, 128, 130, 135,
  144–145, 153, 161–162, 164
  see also: ego, phantasy
  actual, 15, 77
  collective, 78
  culture/cultural, xii, 15, 95, 99, 155,
    161
  external, 53, 167
  human, xiv, 104, 159, 168
  ideal, 160
  laminated, 88
  living, 87
  material, 15, 161
  -motility, 15
  physical, 155
  political, 85
  principle, 77, 129, 144, 161
  psychic, xii, 15, 162
  psychological, 100
  sense of, 77
  social, 79, 87–88, 94, 96, 99–100,
    104, 106, 160
  -thought, 15
  unsatisfying, 77
  -value, 61
  world of, 79
Remotti, F., 159
repression, xii, xvii, 2, 6, 28, 31–32,
  43, 51, 53, 57–60, 66, 72, 76, 81,
  96, 118, 131–132, 136, 143, 145,
  146, 148, 154, 157, 163–164
  desires, 138
  instinctual, 51, 59, 117–118

For Product Safety Concerns and Information please contact our EU
representative GPSR@taylorandfrancis.com
Taylor & Francis Verlag GmbH, Kaufingerstraße 24, 80331 München, Germany

www.ingramcontent.com/pod-product-compliance
Lightning Source LLC
Chambersburg PA
CBHW070330270326
41926CB00017B/3825